Conceptual Foundations of Language Science

No scientific work proceeds without conceptual foundations. In language science, our concepts about language determine our assumptions, direct our attention, and guide our hypotheses and our reasoning. Only with clarity about conceptual foundations can we pose coherent research questions, design critical experiments, and collect crucial data. This series publishes short and accessible books that explore well-defined topics in the conceptual foundations of language science. The series provides a venue for conceptual arguments and explorations that do not require the traditional book-length treatment, yet that demand more space than a typical journal article allows.

In this series:

1. Enfield, N. J. Natural causes of language.
2. Müller, Stefan. A lexicalist account of argument structure: Template-based phrasal LFG approaches and a lexical HPSG alternative.
3. Schmidtke-Bode, Karsten, Natalia Levshina, Susanne Maria Michaelis & Ilja A. Seržant (eds.). Explanation in typology: Diachronic sources, functional motivations and the nature of the evidence.
4. Morley, Rebecca L. Sound structure and sound change: A modeling approach.

ISSN: 2363-877X

Sound structure and sound change

A modeling approach

Rebecca L. Morley

language
science
press

Morley, Rebecca L. 2019. *Sound structure and sound change: A modeling approach* (Conceptual Foundations of Language Science 4). Berlin: Language Science Press.

This title can be downloaded at:
http://langsci-press.org/catalog/book/251

ISBN: 978-3-96110-190-0 (Digital)
978-3-96110-191-7 (Hardcover)

ISSN: 2363-877X
DOI:10.5281/zenodo.3264909
Source code available from www.github.com/langsci/251
Collaborative reading: paperhive.org/documents/remote?type=langsci&id=251

Cover and concept of design: Ulrike Harbort
Typesetting: Felix Kopecky, Rebecca L. Morley
Proofreading: Agnes Kim, Amir Ghorbanpour, Amr Zaway, Carla Bombi, David Lukeš, George Walkden, Ivelina Stoyanova, Ivica Jeđud, Janina Rado, Jean Nitzke, Jeroen van de Weijer, Jezia Talavera, Klara Kim, Laura Arnold, Paulson Skerrit, Steven Moran, Tom Bossuyt
Fonts: Libertinus, Arimo, DejaVu Sans Mono
Typesetting software: XƎLaTeX

Language Science Press
Unter den Linden 6
10099 Berlin, Germany
langsci-press.org

Storage and cataloguing done by FU Berlin

Freie Universität Berlin

Contents

1 Introduction

Synchronic and diachronic linguistics are typically pursued as separate disciplines, with little to no overlap. Nevertheless, it is not possible for either to be truly agnostic about the form of the other. This is necessarily true because synchronic theories are not theories about attested languages, but theories about possible languages. Therefore, any possible language, undergoing any series of diachronic changes, must always end up as another member of the set of possible synchronic languages. Conversely, a theory of the end state of diachronic change is necessarily a theory of a synchronic grammar at some point in time. The actuators of change must also be latently present in some way within synchronic states, just as the speakers of daughter languages must have been learners of mother languages.

In this work I will demonstrate how deeply held assumptions about the correct representations of synchronic grammars delimit an associated theory of diachrony, and how standard assumptions about the units of change disallow certain synchronic states. I will argue that it is necessary to reconsider the operative units within both domains, and that in doing so we are likely to gain new insights into how linguistic structures change and, by extension, how they fail to change, i.e., exhibit stable variation.

The goal of this work is to determine what types of mental structures may be sufficient, and, possibly, necessary in order to capture certain linguistic phenomena at a computational level of description (in the sense of Marr 1982). The approach is twofold: 1) to test a number of proposed structures and mechanisms by implementing them in simple computational models; and 2) to test the explanatory adequacy of a number of existing models by transforming their implementations into theoretical constructs. The first method is likely to be familiar to many readers; the second, however, is somewhat novel, and requires some explanation. In the simplest terms, it is the reverse of the first: taking implemented functions and deriving the theoretical linguistic entity that the function implements. This requires determining whether a specific implementational detail is incidental (with no repercussions beyond the implementational level), or whether there are hidden ramifications to that choice at the level of linguistic theory (the computational level). There is a second aspect to this analysis as well.

Models, to be useful, as well as tractable, must be simplifications of what are extremely complex systems. The simplifications, however, must be of the right kind to ensure that the model is still informative about the phenomenon of interest. That is, the model must be able to "scale up". There is no algorithm, however, by which we can establish scalability ahead of time in building our toy models. Thus, it is critical that any model be made consistent with what is known more globally about the phenomenon of interest (what I will refer to as "imposing boundary conditions"), and not just the small piece it was designed to explain.

As a series of models are developed and tested, they will be assessed as to whether or not they meet the relevant boundary conditions in an internally consistent, theoretically motivated way. This higher-level model analysis will reveal the covert representational corollaries of various modeling choices, providing insight, in turn, into both sufficient and necessary components of a working theory of language stability and change. This approach is also an illustration of the utility of an intensively fine-grained local analysis in approaching the largest and most general of theoretical questions. Although the phenomena modeled are phonetic and phonological ones, the methodology is applicable to any domain of linguistics.

This book is organized as follows. In the remainder of this chapter the representational issues that apply in both the synchronic and the diachronic domains are introduced. Chapter 2 describes the basic architecture from which the models are built. To begin with, three general types of phenomena are modeled: a gradient context-free process, a gradient context-dependent process, and a categorical context-dependent process. Simulations for all three demonstrate that iterated processes without check lead to collapse, or unbounded category shift. Furthermore, production modeled as random selection of unnormalized perceptual inputs leads to sub-category mismatch. Chapter 3 makes explicit links between these general model types and specific linguistic phenomena, namely, word frequency effects, vowel lengthening, and vowel nasalization. In Chapter 4, articulatory targets are introduced to the basic model in order to check unbounded shift. A set of models with targets of various kinds are analyzed in depth. The set is generated by selecting parameters along two dimensions: whether production tokens are stored or generated (STATE/PROCESS); and whether more than one level of representation is used (category/sub-category). In this chapter it is shown that only two models from this set satisfy the criteria of being both representationally consistent and bounded. The possible states for each of the two models is then fully derived. These results are related to existing models, and the types of sound change that they are capable of capturing. In Chapter 5, it is shown that the typical implementational simplification, in which perception and production tokens are equated, is not only implausible, but obscures a fundamental flaw in the mechanism for change. Iterative change no longer follows once an explicit mapping between acoustic values and articulatory gestures is required. Chapter 6 is devoted to a type of change not previously modeled: the genesis of a new phoneme category. Adopting a theory in which the mapping from perception to production is taken to be inherently ambiguous, I offer a proposal for an implemented model in which variable sub-lexical segmentation results in mixed representations. Change in the model is taken to be change in the distribution of already existing variants. The work is summarized in Chapter 7, where other types of sound change, and future avenues of research, are briefly discussed.

1.1 Abstract representations

One of the basic representational divisions that can be made in a theory of cognition is between what is stored in memory versus what is not stored, and thus must be computed (or generated). The choice about what aspects of a linguistic pattern to treat as stored versus generated will determine, to quite a large extent, what we take to be the possible dimensions of synchronic variation cross-linguistically, as well as the possible diachronic outcomes. This will be the focus of Chapter 4, where I will also show that this choice can imply a number of other representational assumptions. In this section, I preview that analysis by deconstructing some of the most basic units of phonological theory.

It should be noted that mainstream synchronic linguistics is heavily biased towards conceptualizing phenomena as generating processes: "vowel nasalization", "final de-voicing", "initial aspiration", etc.[1] This is directly linked to a conception of mental representations as maximally abstract. In other words, only unpredictable information should be stored (such as the arbitrary sound units associated with a given lexical item), while all predictable information should be derived. Although this view may have originated with Chomsky & Halle (1968), it has also been explicitly advocated for much more recently in various theories of underspecification (e.g., Archangeli 1988; Steriade 1995). More commonly, however, it is an unexpressed assumption that the analysis that maximizes the predictive power of the grammar is the preferred one.[2]

For example, the pronunciation of the word *lamb* in English can be written with the following series of phonetic symbols: [læ̃m], where the diacritic over

[1]Even if these are merely terminological conveniences, they color the way we think about, and model, these phenomena.

[2]Within Optimality Theory, this pressure is, in a sense, even stronger, because all possible words must be filtered through the grammar (not just the selected URs). However, Lexicon Optimization allows for known lexical items to be generated from faithful inputs allowing for some predictability to be retained in the lexicon (Prince & Smolensky 2004: Ch. 9).

the vowel indicates nasalization. The property of nasalization, however, is predictable in English, and only occurs when vowels are produced in proximity to nasal consonants, like [m]. The lexical entry for *lamb* is therefore denoted as /læm/, without the nasalization. Concomitantly, a pronunciation rule must be internalized by the native English speaker, a rule that stipulates that any vowels adjacent to nasal consonants must become nasalized. Under this theory, the lexical item /læm/ is first retrieved, and then transformed to [læ̃m] via the application of this rule.

This hypothesis in fact implies that the lexical entry is comprised of a string of smaller units, the phonemes /l/, /æ/, and /m/, that are concatenated together in order to produce the word. The currently standard view of phonological structure is that there exists an entire hierarchy of abstract units wherein larger units are successively built from smaller ones: phonemes from features, syllables from phonemes, words from syllables, etc. At each level, the units of the previous level undergo rules affecting their realization. The unit of interest in a particular analysis will depend on the phenomenon of interest. But that unit cannot exist independently of the rest of the hierarchy. Consider the dual nature of the phoneme /æ/ as part of an abstract category /æ/, but also as part of the word *lamb*. The variant, or allophone, of the phoneme that occurs in that word is nasalized. However, the rule that nasalizes the /æ/ is assumed to operate at a more abstract level, i.e., before any nasal, in any word and, in fact, on any vowel. See (1.1).

(1.1) */vowel/ → [nasalized vowel]/__ [nasal]*

Many phonemes can be said to have multiple phonological allophones, and all phonemes have at least multiple phonetic allophones. In the word *tag* [tʰæˑg̚], for example, the first sound can be characterized as the aspirated allophone of /t/ that is generated whenever a voiceless plosive occurs in the onset of a stressed syllable; the second sound is the lengthened allophone of /æ/ that is generated whenever a vowel precedes a voiced obstruent; and the third sound is the unreleased allophone of /g/ that is generated whenever a plosive occurs in word-final position.

A consequence of abstract representations that do not match produced surface forms is that a normalization procedure is required on the perception side for successful recognition and retrieval. The actually heard [læ̃m] does not match the stored representation /læm/, and must be converted by somehow subtracting out, or "compensating" for, the predictable nasality. As far as I am aware, there is no standard notation for formalizing the input (or perception) side of the allophonic relationship. Therefore, I use the special symbol ↪ to denote the inference of the underlying form in (1.2), the inverse of (1.1).

(1.2) *[nasalized vowel][nasal] ↪ /vowel//nasal/*

Once performed, the recovered form should be identical to the stored category. Thus, from the generative perspective, category matching is trivial, and the difficult part of speech recognition is the normalization process. Note that the more rules there are, and the more complex their interaction, the more complicated the normalization procedure becomes.[3]

1.2 Actuation

A commonly described sound change is one in which a sound that was previously an allophone becomes a phoneme in its own right (phoneme split). Vowel nasalization is considered to be allophonic in English, and was also allophonic at some point in the history of French. The allophonic rule entailed that a word like /bɔn/ would be pronounced as [bɔ̃n]. According to the classical view, loss of nasal consonants like the one in [bɔ̃n], resulted in words like [bɔ̃], where the nasalized variant was no longer predictable (e.g., Hajek 1997). In theory, a minimal pair was now possible where the only difference between the word pairs was whether the vowel was oral or nasal, e.g., [bɔ̃] versus [bɔ].

This story creates a paradox within the constraints of the representational framework just described. If nasalization is predictable, then it is added by rule to an abstract underlying form, such as /bɔn/. If the final nasal is dropped by the speaker, then there should be no nasalization on the vowel, and no way to arrive at a phonemically nasalized vowel.[4] If the final nasal is not dropped by the speaker, but fails to be heard by the listener, a different problem arises. A listener provided with the input sequence [bɔ̃] ought to infer, based on their native language competence, that they failed to hear a nasal consonant that was actually produced, given that vowels are only ever nasalized preceding a nasal consonant. In fact, they ought to be able to infer, based on the conversational

[3] The real speech perception problem, of course, is much more difficult than simply accounting for all the phonetic and phonological predictability. There are numerous other factors that affect the realization of a given utterance, such as vocal tract length, speaking rate, ambient noise, speaker sex, speech community, register, etc. At minimum, normalization of all these factors requires a complex non-linear function, and is unlikely to have a unique solution.

[4] In fact, it is possible to achieve the necessary outcome if the nasal is dropped by the speaker only *after* the allophonic rule has been applied. This move, however, requires a theory of serially ordered rules in the first place, and, in the second, raises other difficulties in terms of theoretical constraints on the ordering of those rules, and what types of rules are allowed to occur before or after others.

context and their knowledge of lexical items, that the target was *bon*, and thus correct for any performance errors in production or perception.

The causality in this story can be reversed, where the loss of the nasal, rather than being the actuating event, merely reveals (to the linguist) that the nasalized vowel has already become phonemic (e.g., Janda & Joseph 2003). This "covert change" approach, however, merely pushes the explanation back a step – how did the vowel become phonemically nasal? And in either story the Actuation Problem (Weinreich et al. 1968) remains unsolved. What is required is a mechanism by which predictability can be lost at the allophonic level. Furthermore, the mechanism itself must be predictable; that is, it must either always apply (yet only occasionally lead to sound change), or it must apply under specific well-understood conditions.

1.3 Less-abstract representations

Even within a maximally abstract system it will be necessary to deal with multiple representational levels in a way that is obscured by the notational conventions used above. For example, a phoneme split was said to require predictability to be lost at the allophonic level. But, in fact, what is really needed is the loss of predictability at a hyper-allophonic level, such as that expressed in (1.1) – which will be symbolized as $[\tilde{V}]$ going forward. And because neither phonemes, allophones, or hyper-allophones exist in isolation, whatever mechanism is proposed must act through the medium of actual words. Furthermore, sound change has been observed to be gradual from a phonetic point of view, such that relatively small differences in pronunciation can be seen to incrementally increase across speakers of different ages in a "sound change in progress". These small differences are reflected in what may be stable differences between different dialects, between male and female speakers, between speakers of higher socioeconomic and lower socioeconomic status, etc. It is now widely accepted, in fact, that the pool of phonetic variants that exists across a heterogeneous population of speakers provides the basis for future sound changes (e.g., Guy 2008).

For these reasons, an alternative framework in which mental representations are far closer to actually produced forms, retaining significant detail at both the acoustic and phonetic levels, has arisen in the study of sound change. Exemplar models were first developed in the field of psychology, in order to reflect a number of insights about human memory and categorization. Rather than having clear, definable boundaries, many mental categories seemed to function much more as though they were a reflection of their current members (e.g., Rosch 1977). Categorization of novel items was less a question of logical inference, than of similarity to known instances. Furthermore, many dimensions of similarity were potentially implicated, not all of which were relevant from a taxonomic point of view (Nosofsky 1988; Luce 1986). Within linguistics, exemplar models have been invoked to account for a host of factors known to affect both word recognition and production, but which are not expressable within a maximally abstract generative framework. Among these are the pervasive effects of word frequency (Bybee 2001), the familiar-speaker effect in word priming, as well as the persistence of sub-phonemic detail (Tilsen 2009), and the influence of socio-indexical variables on what are typically assumed to be more abstract, grammatical levels of processing (see Docherty & Foulkes 2014 for review).

The term "exemplar" is meant to indicate that representations being stored in memory are of individual, specific experiences. For example, each time you hear the word *lamb* over the course of your lifetime, spoken by any of a number of different people, in any number of different contexts, an exemplar that resides within the category associated with the word *lamb* is created. Just as a minimal representational framework implies the necessity of a normalization procedure, a "maximal" representational framework suggests that normalization of the acoustic signal may not be necessary at all. Since previous experiences of the word *lamb* share many similarities, among them that fact that that there is some degree of nasalization on the vowel, they are likely to provide the closest matches to any new token that also contains a nasalized vowel of this type. No reversal of nasalization is required (cf. Johnson 1997). Classification occurs by discovering the cloud to which a new token bears the closest over-all similarity in this space. However, because speech is so variable, in ways that listeners seem quite sensitive to, this mental space is a very high-dimensional one. As a result, the similarity computation is likely to be quite complex.

Because the relationship between the acoustic speech signal and the structural units of language is a non-linear, many-to-many mapping, there must always be a theoretical trade-off of this kind. For an easy classification algorithm, generative theory requires complex pre-processing in the form of a normalization procedure. For little to no pre-processing, exemplar theory requires a complex classification algorithm. In the modeling work that follows we will adopt the non-trivial assumption that classification is perfect – that all tokens are recognized as members of their intended category. The complexity, however, will surface in the transformation between what is perceived (and subsequently stored), and what is produced (based on what is stored). Nominally, all the models in this work are exemplar models. However, they are really much more general-purpose models. In the limit, all tokens can belong to a single category, or all categories contain a single token each. The question of normalization will remain central because it depends on exactly how abstract the representations are, and there will always be a trade-off between what is stored and what is computed.

2 The basic model

One of the earliest exemplar models within linguistics, Goldinger (1996) (adapting Hintzman 1984), was designed to capture the effect of past experience on current perception. In this model, new tokens are experienced and added to memory in the following way. First, the n-dimensional similarity between a novel ("probe") token and all members of a given category is calculated. The overall degree of similarity will determine whether a given probe is recognized or not. The similarity matrix is, in turn, used to create an "echo" of the probe: the average of the values of each stored token, along each dimension, weighted by the similarity of that token to the probe. This echo, rather than the probe itself, is what is then added to memory. These properties allow the model to simulate the phenomenon whereby listeners often mistakenly "remember" tokens that are particularly "good", or prototypical, members of a category, even when they have never actually experienced those tokens. Goldinger's model also introduced a production component – a seemingly minimal extension in which a stored echo can be selected for "readout". Goldinger is explicit about assuming that the articulations needed to produce a given auditory token can be accurately reconstructed from the acoustics of that token (and thus directly "read out" from the stored perception token). This assumption would be implicitly adopted in most of the work that followed.

2.1 Feedback loop

The standard perception-production loop model, as well as the application to sound change *per se*, appears to have originated with Pierrehumbert (2001). Production in this model starts with random selection from a store of perceived tokens. Each production, in turn, is then perceived (either by the original speaker, or by an interlocutor with an identical exemplar space) and then stored. Then the process begins again. In this way, small perturbations (noise or articulatory biases in production; perceptual biases or error in perception) accumulate in the exemplar cloud, leading to gradual shifts in the category as a whole. The perception-production loop that will form the basis for the models discussed in this book is schematized in Figure 2.1.

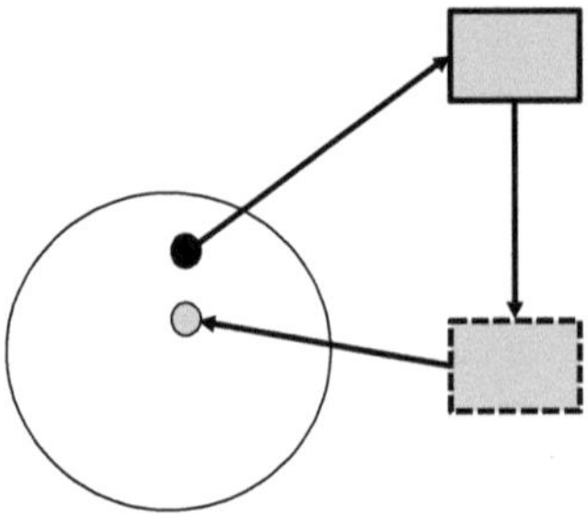

Figure 2.1: Perception-Production Feedback Loop

The basic exemplar model includes three additional mechanisms that are necessary for generating useful results. The first of these is what is typically conceptualized as an error term. This allows for variation to persist, and provides the necessary stochastic element needed for achieving multiple outcomes. The second is entrenchment, which prevents categories from losing cohesion and dispersing along the dimensions of variation. The third mechanism is memory decay, privileging more recent perceptions in memory, and preventing the category from simply getting larger and larger. Figure 2.2 is a schematic of the basic algorithm for the models that will be implemented and run below. Mathematical details will be provided in the following section and the Appendices.

2.2 Entrenchment

Category consolidation, or variance reduction, has been motivated as an effect of practice, or motor tuning (e.g. Saltzman & Munhall 1989). Implementationally, it is necessary to prevent the category expansion in both directions that would result from consistent production error, and the additional expansion that would occur in the biasing direction. The general equation for entrenchment that will be used in this paper is the following (based on Pierrehumbert 2001):

(2.1) $$E(x_i) = \epsilon(\bar{x} - x_i)$$

where ϵ is a constant between 0 and 1, x_i is the current location of token i along some dimension x, and $\overline{x}$ is the current category mean along that dimension. Figure 2.3 illustrates the evolution of a single exemplar cloud generated from the model outlined in Figure 2.2. In each sub-figure the different colors indicate the same distribution at initialization (white), and after a certain fixed number of

Baseline Perception-Production Model (one dimensional)

(a) Initialize cloud
   - assign values to a cloud of n tokens (randomly generated from a normal distribution of mean μ and variance σ^2)
   - assign each token an age (a time at which it was produced)

(b) Randomly select a token for production
   - add the production bias, moving the token a small amount in the biasing direction
   - add the error term, moving the token a small amount in either direction
   - add entrenchment, moving the token a small amount closer to the category mean

(c) Store
   - add the new token value to the cloud
   - remove one of the oldest tokens from the cloud

(d) Return to Step (b)

Figure 2.2: Baseline Model Specification

model iterations (black). Unless otherwise stated, all models are assumed to be one-dimensional along x. Individual tokens are given as counts over successively binned x values.

Figure 2.3a shows how the distribution as a whole shifts in the direction of the production bias over time (measured in iterations of the perception-production loop). Figure 2.3b shows the result of running the same model, minus the entrenchment term, over the same number of iterations. The biasing shift still occurs, but with increasing variance along the biased dimension. See Appendix A for the specific parameter values used in these, and the following, simulations.

2.3 Memory decay

Without memory decay, categories can only spread without shifting. The older the tokens, the more times, on average, they will have been chosen as production targets, reinforcing the initial conditions of the cloud. Figure 2.3c is an illustration of this effect for the same model and starting conditions as the previous two simulations, but with the memory decay term removed. No tokens were discarded. The skew in the direction of the production bias (implemented as an incrementally decreasing function) can be seen in the left tail of the distribution, but older tokens keep the category anchored at the right. There are a number of ways in which a memory decay term can be implemented. In these and the following models, the total number of tokens is kept constant by removing one of the oldest tokens each time a new token is added.[1]

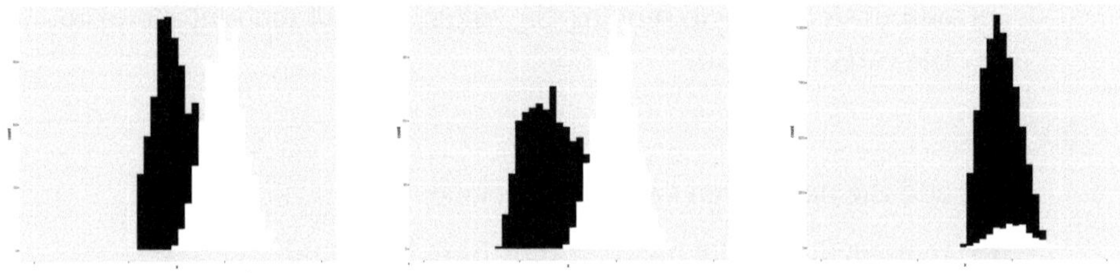

(a) All Forces (b) Without Entrenchment (c) Without Memory Decay

Figure 2.3: Basic Iterative Model: Starting distribution (white); Distribution after 8000 iterations (black). Note that y-axis range in c) is about 10 times larger than in a) and b).

2.4 The collapse problem

As illustrated in Figure 2.3a, the basic exemplar model with a single unidirectional bias can produce cohesive movement of an entire cloud of exemplars in the direction of the bias. What will be demonstrated in this section is that this shift is unbounded, leading ultimately to category collapse and merger. This could easily be inferred from the fact that the basic model contains only one force that acts in a consistent direction, with nothing to oppose it. However, it is worthwhile to

[1]There are other ways to keep the number of category members constant. The token furthest from the mean could be discarded on each iteration, for example. This would act to increase the entrenchment effect, further reducing variation. However, the purpose here is not only to keep the number of tokens constant, but to allow a domino effect to develop by increasing the probability that a token will be chosen again with each biasing iteration.

actually run the simulations for a number of reasons. Unambiguously establishing the results for general classes of phenomena will allow us to see immediately what the model predicts for the linguistic phenomena that map to each of those classes. Running actual simulations will also force us to consider the question of whether exemplar models are to be evaluated only at convergence, and what the relationship is between model time and real time, in terms of experiences of instances of speech. Finally, the specific ways in which the models fail will be informative regarding the mental representations they are meant to instantiate.

The three classes of phenomena to be modeled in this section are the following: a context-free process; and two context-dependent processes, one gradient, and one categorical. For all of the three basic models, a production bias, *B*, will be implemented for a given token *i*, as a fixed percentage reduction (α) in the value of x_i along dimension *x*. See Eq. (2.2).[2]

(2.2) $$B(x_i) = -x_i\alpha$$

After the production bias applies, the biased token will be added back to the cloud from which it was originally drawn. It will be useful to express the value of a given token on any iteration as a function of the original non-biased token that gave rise to it. For one such original token, x_i, we can label its biased daughter as $x_{i(+1)}$, and calculate its biased value to be $x_i(1-\alpha)$ along dimension *x*. If, on some subsequent iteration, this daughter token $x_{i(+1)}$ is chosen for production, it will be subject to the same biasing force, resulting in the granddaughter, $x_{i(+2)}$, with value $x_{i(+2)} = x_{i(+1)}(1-\alpha) = x_i(1-\alpha)^2$. Proceeding to the general case, we can express the value of any token, on any given model iteration, as a function of the value of its originator token (x_o), and the number of generations, *n*, by which the current token is removed from that originator. See Eq. (2.3).

(2.3) $$x_{o(+n)} = x_o\,(1-\alpha)^n$$

2.4.1 Model 1: Context-free iterativity

In Model 1, the bias function applies to all tokens. Therefore, the linear bias term in (2.3) will cause the entire category to shift in the biasing direction over time. The following simulations compare the behavior of a low-frequency category,

[2] The production bias in Pierrehumbert (2001) is a constant that applies regardless of the current token value. Making the bias proportional results in less reduction for tokens that already have small values, thus fixing the percentage of reduction, rather than the absolute value, for all tokens.

to a high-frequency category, one whose tokens are produced, and thus experienced, more often. All simulations begin with the same starting distributions: a high-frequency category with 800 tokens, and a low-frequency category with 200 tokens. Steps were taken to make the distributions of the two categories as close as possible.[3] See Figure 2.4.

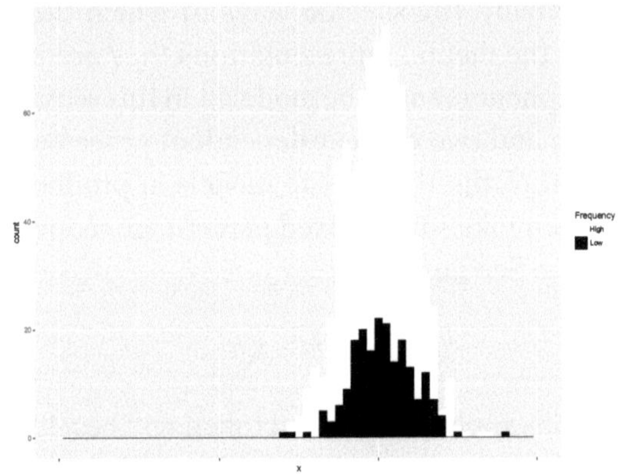

Figure 2.4: Starting Distribution. White bars: High-frequency category. Black bars: Low-frequency category.

Because these models rely on random processes, the outcome is not guaranteed to be identical each time the model is run. To evaluate models of this kind, one conducts a number of independent identical "experiments" (trials) that consist of running the model with the same starting conditions, and the same parameters, for the same number of iterations. Results are then averaged over the set of trials. In the first set of simulations, 500 model trials were run for 1000 iterations each. On each model iteration one token was produced, selected stochastically from among all possible tokens (making it 4 times more likely to be chosen from the high-frequency than the low-frequency category). That token was biased according to Eq. (2.2) and then added back to the category from which it originated.

The mean category value along x for each category was calculated at the end of each of the 500 trials, and converted to a z-score. A boxplot of the difference between the means of the two categories on each trial is shown in Figure 2.5a. In 44% of trials the difference was negative (low-frequency mean larger than

[3]The high-frequency category was generated by randomly sampling 800 tokens from a normal distribution with mean of $50x$ and a standard deviation of $2x$. The low-frequency category was then created by sampling 200 tokens from the high-frequency category: 50 tokens from each quartile.

high-frequency), and in 56% it was positive. The mean difference over all 500 trials was close to zero: 0.031 (or 16% of the initial distribution standard deviation). Thus we do not see a consistent difference in the two categories after an arbitrarily selected number of iterations. Intuitively, we might have expected the higher-frequency category to have moved further along x, and have a lower value, because tokens from that category are produced more often, and thus multiply-biased. However, it is also the case that, if frequency of occurrence is expressed in number of tokens, and sampling for production is random, then producing a token that had undergone biasing *fewer* times is also more likely in high than in low frequency categories. This is simply because there are more tokens, which lowers the probability of selecting any individual token, and thus lowers the probability of selecting the daughter of any individual token, relative to the low-frequency category.

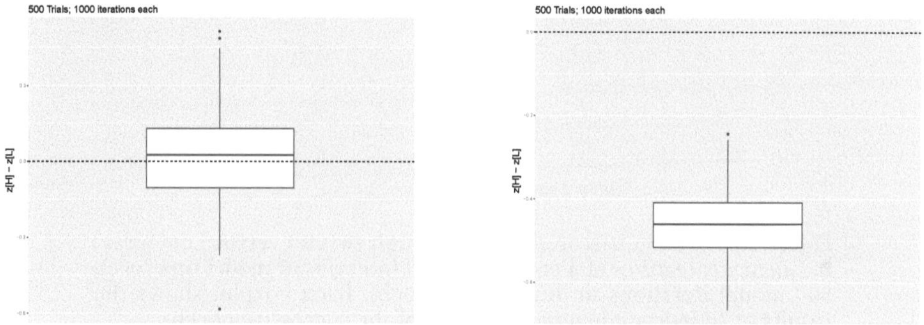

(a) 4:1 Token ratio (b) 1:1 Token Ratio

Figure 2.5: Simulation of Iterative Biasing for H(igh) frequency category versus L(ow) frequency category

The difference in the number of tokens in each category also results in a difference in variance across the different trials. The variance is larger for the lower-frequency category due to undersampling; because fewer tokens are produced from the low-frequency category in a given trial, and the tokens are selected randomly, the likelihood that the sample will be significantly different from trial to trial is greater (Sóskuthy 2014 finds a similar effect using a parameterized exemplar model). Variance compounds over iterations, such that the variance between independent model runs after 10,000 iterations is greater than after 5000 iterations. Figure 2.6 illustrates the across-trial variance for the two categories at successive intervals, after 500, 1000, 1500, and 2000 iterations.

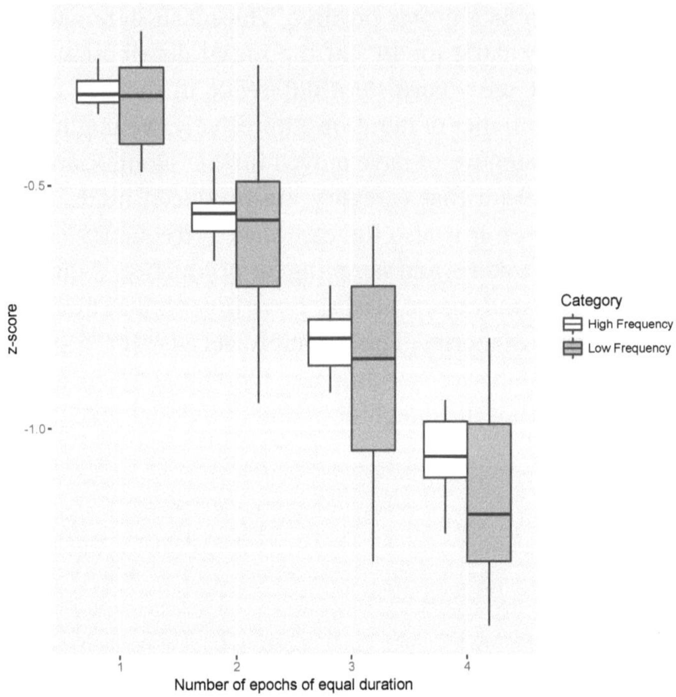

Figure 2.6: Average z-scored value for High (white) versus Low (gray) frequency categories at 4 equally spaced intervals of model time, each 500 model iterations in duration (1 epoch). Each boxplot shows the results of 10 independent trials at each of the successive epochs.

Different implementational choices and assumptions will produce somewhat different results. If the two categories contain the same constant number of tokens, but the high-frequency category is still 4 times more likely to be produced on any given iteration, then the high-frequency category will have a consistently lower value along x than the low-frequency category. The results of the equal-tokens simulations are shown in Figure 2.5b. This is because the inertia from the larger number of few-times-biased tokens is missing. These specific results also depend on the ratio of frequencies of the two categories, as well as a number of other parameter settings. Those dependencies will be discussed further in Section 3.1, when this model is linked to the linguistic phenomenon of frequency-based word reduction. For now, I turn to the behavior of the model in the limit.

The means of both categories steadily decrease as a function of the number of model iterations. Although the amount of biasing becomes steadily smaller as token values become smaller, biasing is unbounded. That is, the model does not converge on a stable state. Convergence can be imposed by specifying a minimum value on x beyond which tokens cannot be reduced. This results in a skewed distribution with a narrow peak at the threshold value and a small rightward tail due to the normally distributed error term. The thresholded model clearly illustrates that all categories, whether high or low frequency, will eventually end up at exactly the same minimum value, collapsing any difference between them.

2.4.2 Context-dependent iterativity

In the previous model all tokens of each category were subjected to the same production bias – the context in which the tokens were produced did not matter. The next two models are context-dependent models. In these models the production bias only applies to a subset of tokens, those produced in the biasing context. As before, production tokens are chosen at random; they are then produced in either a biasing or non-biasing context, with a certain fixed probability. Regardless of production context, however, all tokens are added back to the same originating category.

2.4.2.1 Model 2: Gradient context-dependent bias

Model 2 implements a gradient production bias, similar to the one used in Model 1, but with an increasing, rather than decreasing, function of x. On each iteration, the randomly selected token has probability p (< 0.5) of increasing by a fixed percentage (α) of its current value. As before, the category is initialized by sampling from a normal distribution, and all tokens begin with non-biased values. Because there is only one cloud in perception, the only time a difference between biased and non-biased tokens can be observed is at the moment of production. Therefore, model outputs will be given in terms of an observed random sample of fixed size at some cycle, n, of the model.

The iterativity of the perception-production loop allows for tokens to be biased multiple times, but also for tokens to remain persistently non-biased, the more so the larger the category is in terms of stored exemplars, and the smaller the value of p. To understand model behavior it is useful to think of each iteration as involving four possible outcomes. In the first, a relatively low-valued token (the outcome of a series of productions occurring more often in non-biasing contexts) is chosen for production, but this time in a biasing context, thus increasing its value along x. The second possibility is that the same token is chosen for production in a non-biasing context, such that its value remains more or less unchanged (still relatively low). The third and fourth possibilities involve selecting a relatively high-valued token (the outcome of a series of productions occurring more often in the biasing context) and either producing it in a non-biasing context (no increase along x), or a biasing context (additional increase along x).

The last type of outcome ensures that a subset of tokens will continue to increase without bound. Despite the fact that the second type of outcome ensures the persistence of low-valued tokens, the category as a whole will move unboundedly rightward along x. This is due to the combined effect of memory decay and entrenchment. For $p < 0.5$, the overall mean of the distribution will always be closer to the lower-valued side of the distribution, and will initially act to oppose the increase due to production bias. However, as higher-valued tokens are added to the category, they seed even higher-valued daughter tokens, generating an exponentially increasing subset of tokens. This is the relationship expressed in Eq. (2.3), reformulated here, for a positive bias, as $x_{o(+n)} = x_o(1 + \alpha)$. As this subset of tokens moves right, it will drag the rest of the distribution with it. Figure 2.7 illustrates this effect via comparison of the observed distribution after a model run of 1,000 iterations, versus 5,000 iterations.

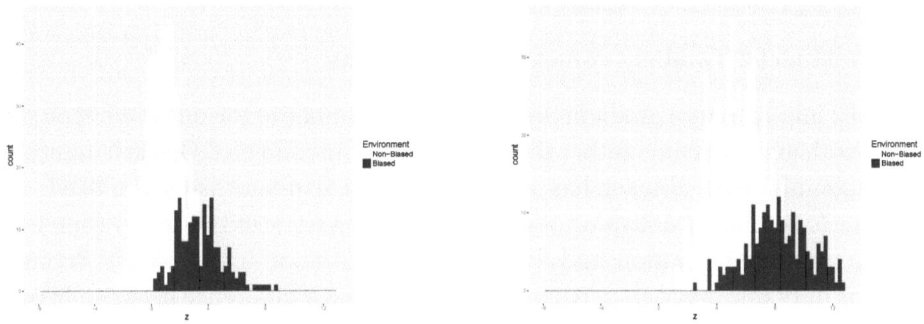

(a) 1000 iterations

(b) 5000 iterations

Figure 2.7: Observed distribution (800 tokens). White: productions in non-biasing context. Black: productions in biasing context.

As expected, the same unboundedness problem arises as was seen in Model 1. With the addition of a threshold (ceiling or floor value along x) the sub-distributions merge, neutralizing the difference between biased and non-biased contexts.[4] It will also be shown that keeping all tokens in the same category, regardless of history, results in another type of problem – what I will call context mismatch. Context mismatch will be discussed when this model is linked to the linguistic phenomenon of vowel lengthening in Section 3.2.

[4]Tupper (2014) attributes a merged outcome such as this to perfect categorization accuracy, i.e., failure to discard ambiguous tokens.

2.4.2.2 Model 3: Categorical context-dependent bias

Model 3 implements a binary production bias, albeit with an error term that maintains a small amount of variance. All tokens produced in the biasing context are initialized with a mean at the [+] value on dimension *x*, while all tokens produced in the non-biasing context are initialized at the [–] value. See Figure 2.8a. As before, all tokens belong to the same category; the different colors are for illustrative purposes only, allowing us to track the production context during the observation cycle. Because the bias is uni-directional, and biasing is categorical, all tokens quickly shift to the biased [+] value. Once a token has a value of /+/ it cannot be biased further, nor can it be "un-biased". This is shown in Figure 2.8b, where we can see that previously biased tokens remain at [+] even if they are subsequently produced in a non-biasing context (white bars at [+] location). This model is, in fact, bounded, because there is no iterativity for the binary feature. However, like the previous two models, it results in neutralization of the difference between the different contexts. Binary-valued features that distinguish between contrastive sound units within a language are widely used in phonological theory. This connection will be discussed when the model is linked to the linguistic phenomenon of vowel nasalization in Section 3.3.

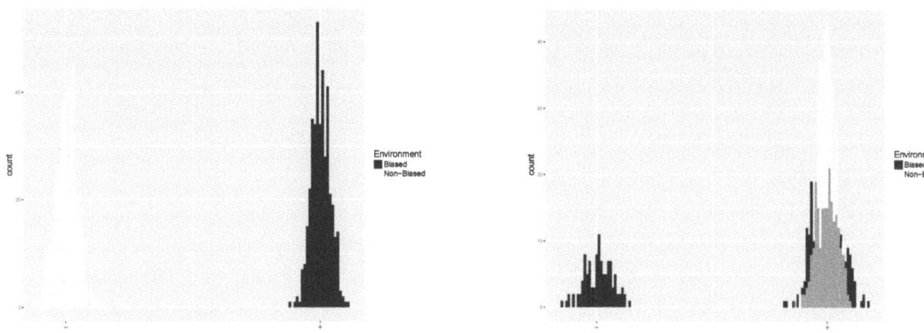

(a) Starting Distribution

(b) 1000 iterations

Figure 2.8: Quasi-binary feature. Two variants with equal contextual frequency.

3 The linguistic phenomena

The general context-free and context-dependent processes modeled in the previous chapter will now be mapped to specific linguistic phenomena. This chapter will show more concretely what the implementational and conceptual issues are in developing exemplar models based on tokens of experienced speech. I will also begin to examine the proper interpretation of model results with respect to existing theories and, conversely, the proper implementation of specific theoretical hypotheses within an exemplar framework.

3.1 Model 1: Word frequency

In laboratory speech, as well as spoken corpora, it has been repeatedly demonstrated that words that are more commonly used are shorter in duration than comparable words that are less common (e.g., Bybee 2001; 2002; 2006). Furthermore, it has been shown that as frequency increases, the average duration of a given word monotonically decreases (controlling for other factors). The diachronic counterpart of this phenomenon is the observation that more frequent words tend to "lead", meaning that a change that will later spread throughout all, or most, words of a language is first observed to take place in high-frequency words (e.g., Phillips 1984). Such changes are often themselves reductive in nature, either being the direct result of, or influenced by, a reduction in the temporal, and/or spatial, extent of the articulation of the given sounds (such as segment shortening, segment loss, assimilatory feature changes, or feature centralization).

Competing explanations for frequency-based reduction can be separated into listener-based and speaker-based approaches. In the former, more reduced forms are assumed to be easier/more efficient for speakers to produce, and are thus hypothesized to be the default production mode. However, in the case where the meaning is unclear, or there is greater than normal ambiguity, the speaker exerts more effort in articulation, lengthening and strengthening speech sounds in order to facilitate speech recognition for the listener (e.g., Aylett & Turk 2004). Because words that are highly predictable in context are easier to recover, such words can be safely reduced, whereas less predictable words must be produced more carefully. In the absence of other factors, the marginal probability of a given word provides an estimate of its likelihood; thus low-frequency words will be produced with less reduction in order to facilitate their recovery relative to high-frequency words. A speaker-based approach, on the other hand, attributes frequency effects to automatic consequences of speech production. Either high-frequency words have higher resting activation levels on average, leading to faster retrieval, and thus more rapid articulation (e.g., Gahl et al. 2012), or increased practice with higher-frequency words leads to greater fluency, resulting in shorter, more efficient articulation (e.g., Bybee 2002).

Pierrehumbert (2001) adopts a speaker-based motivation for reduction, modeling the effect as a production bias that shortens each token by the same small fixed amount whenever it is produced. Although a model containing both high and low frequency categories was not actually implemented in Pierrehumbert (2001), the paper suggests that this simple bias can account both for synchronic differences in word duration, as well as reductive changes, over time.

The more often tokens are produced from a given category, the more chances there will be for initially unreduced tokens to be reduced multiple times. Thus, it might seem to follow that higher-frequency categories will shift further leftward than lower-frequency categories over the same period of time. However, as we saw in Section 2.4.1, the relative average durations of a lower- and higher-frequency word category depend on whether the frequency difference is implemented as a difference in token numbers, or a difference in average activation. Furthermore, given enough time (= number of productions), all categories will end up at the same minimum duration. In other words, the model will converge on this one stable state from any starting point. This is the inevitable result of a model with an unopposed force acting, and thus is not particularly surprising (Baker et al. 2011 make a similar observation about gradual-accumulation theories of change in general). However, it raises an important issue regarding the determination of synchronic versus diachronic time in exemplar models.

Computational models are typically only evaluated at convergence. This is in part because there is usually no explicit theory about how time within a model corresponds to real time (or to time in some other model). Exemplar models, however, explicitly map iterations to real-world events, namely, the perception and storage of speech tokens. This requires that literally any stage of the model be a possible synchronic state – at least an instantaneous one. This property also makes it possible, in principle, that the state of the model at convergence (or the fact that the model fails to converge) is irrelevant to evaluation. This is the case if it can be shown that convergence does not occur within the lifetime of the speaker. If the model parameters are chosen in a specific way, collapse may be avoidable within whatever is taken to be an average lifetime. An illustration of what is required to determine these parameters is provided in Appendix B. This line of enquiry uncovers a further prediction of this general model. It must be the case that all words become more reduced over time, regardless of the specific parameter values.

The iterative model strongly implies that the frequency effect must arise in the lifetime of the speaker, and only after they have had sufficient exposure to a given (high frequency) category. I will define this timespan as the time it takes a category of some frequency f, with a reduction bias of α, to reach a degree of reduction, δ_{n_f}, that is expressed as a proportion of the original duration. I will call this amount of real time an epoch, and I will define the number of productions of category f during an epoch as n_f. Then, by definition:

$$\overline{d_{n_f}} = \overline{d_0} - \delta_{n_f}\overline{d_0}.$$

Since we know that a frequency effect is observable, at minimum, in young adults, this epoch cannot be longer than around 20 years. Unless f decreases drastically (in fact, we might expect it to increase at this life stage), then multiple epochs remain in the lives of these speakers, and a decrease comparable to the original frequency effect should be expected to occur in each one of them. Thus, we should find that word durations should get steadily shorter over the lifetime. Of course, there is a hard limit on how much a word can be reduced. If I predict that some words will hit this limit within the given time frame then the frequency effect should actually be lost in the subset of words that have reached this limit. I am not aware of any evidence that frequency effects vary over time, but this lack may be due to the fact that previous studies have not specifically looked for such effects.

3.2 Model 2: Vowel lengthening

Context-dependence is the norm in language, especially in the domain of sound structure. Speech sounds exist in a high-dimensional space, and almost any change in context produces some measurable difference in a sound's pronunciation along one of those dimensions. These effects, however, are usually predictable, and so can be modeled using a fixed bias. Vowel lengthening before voiced obstruents in word-final position provides a simple instantiation of a context-dependent phenomenon that applies to the duration dimension. It has been noted for well over a 100 years that vowels before final voiced obstruents in

English are "very long" (Sweet 1880: 59), and laboratory studies have consistently found significant vowel duration differences between voiced-voiceless minimal pairs like *bad* and *bat* (e.g., Peterson & Lehiste 1960; Chen 1970). Furthermore, perceptual experiments find that vowel duration is a sufficient cue to the "voicing" on the final obstruent, whether that segment is actually voiced or not (e.g., Raphael 1972; Klatt 1976). As it is conventionally described, vowel lengthening is an allophonic process whereby vowels produced in the lengthening context (before voiced obstruents) are lengthened by some degree, while vowels not produced in the lengthening context remain unchanged.

However, the results of the Model 2 simulation show that, over time, "short" tokens get longer, and "long" tokens get even longer, and eventually all tokens are maximally long whether they're produced in pre-voiced or pre-voiceless contexts. Furthermore, it is not possible to guarantee, at any intermediate stage, that tokens produced in the biasing (voiced) context will be consistently longer than tokens produced in the non-biasing (voiceless) context. Because of the different possible histories of each token, the single category contains both tokens that are very long (all ancestors produced in biasing context), and very short (all ancestors produced in non-biasing contexts). If a particularly short token is chosen (at random) for production in a voiced context it won't be as long, even after lengthening, as other tokens in that context have been in the past (on previous iterations). Likewise, if a particularly long token is chosen to be produced in a voiceless context it will be longer than other tokens in that context have tended to be. We know that listeners develop expectations about what they should be hearing based on context, and can detect when the variant differs from expectation (e.g., Krakow et al. 1988; Gaskell & Marslen-Wilson 1996). This mismatch between token and context is therefore a problem for the basic exemplar model.

However, all these effects can be seen to arise out of the fact that all tokens are taken from, and added back to, the same undifferentiated cloud. If tokens of the two allophones were stored separately, then these problems could presumably be eliminated. Let us consider what that would entail. From the perspective of theoretical linguistics, allophones, by definition, have no independent representational status. They exist only at the surface, only as the realization of a phoneme to which some rule, or process, has applied.[1] We are perfectly free to

[1]Note that this model is entirely implemented at the phoneme level, allowing the presumed forces to act directly on their targets. Although exemplar models often assume a word-level representation (explicitly or implicitly), most are actually implemented at the phoneme level, and lack explicit mechanisms for connecting the two (although see Wedel (2012) for a model of an indirect biasing relationship). Mechanisms such as frequency-based reduction and contrast maintenance are defined with respect to the word level. Implementing them at the sub-lexical

adopt the hypothesis that allophones do, in fact, have separate representational status, and create a model in which "lengthened" allophones are only selected from the "lengthened" (sub) category, and only "unlengthened" allophones from the "unlengthened" (sub) category.[2] This would eliminate the context-mismatch problem. A paradox arises, however, if we continue to apply the lengthening bias to the lengthened tokens. By creating a category for these allophones we are effectively encoding their context: this category consists of tokens that occur before voiced obstruents. Applying lengthening to such a token implies that the token was originally unlengthened (non-biased). It also implies that the contextual information was discarded when the token was stored, and so must be added during production. A model with both explicit representational structure incorporating a biasing context, and an actual biasing process, is a strange hybrid. This incompatibility between modeling a phenomenon as both stored *and* generated will be discussed in more depth in Chapter 4.

3.3 Model 3: Vowel nasalization

While phonemes are taken to be the basic phonological unit for many purposes, most phonological rules that operate at the level of individual phonemes, in fact, affect only a subset of that phoneme's features. Classically, phonemes are taken to be decomposable into a universal set of discrete features, and can be uniquely defined by a specific matrix of values over those features. These features are usually assumed not just to be discrete, but to be binary in nature, taking on only one of two possible values, [+] or [−]. Thus a partial feature matrix might consist of

$$\begin{bmatrix} -nasal \\ +coronal \\ -del.rel \end{bmatrix},$$

for example, which matches the phonemes /t/, /d/ and /s/, among others. Whether considered to be phonetic or phonological, nasalization is a process

level not only obscures the fact that a mapping between the levels is necessary, but eliminates a fundamental property of abstraction: the more abstract the unit, the larger the category, and the more, and more varied, the tokens. The phoneme category /æ/ encompasses more than just tokens extracted from the words *tag* and *tack*, but from a large number of words, such as *cat*, *lack*, *sag*, *package*, etc. Any changes at the level of the individual word are only one small part of what affects the realization of a given phoneme. Thus, establishing that a phoneme-level effect follows from a word-level interaction requires a significantly more complex model than is usually implemented.

[2]This is implemented as the State Model in Chapter 4.

that changes the [−*nasal*] specification to [+*nasal*]. In English this rule applies to all vowels occurring in the context of a following nasal consonant (e.g., [læb] vs. [læ̃m]). Thus it is analogous, in all respects other than binarity, to the vowel lengthening example simulated in Model 2, and similarly results in context mismatch. What Model 3 demonstrates more transparently, however, is that the eventual outcome is neutralization of the distinction between the two allophones. Once a given token is produced in a nasal context for the first time, all its daughter tokens will also be nasal, even when produced in an oral context ([læ̃b]). Neutralization occurs because the process of nasalization is uni-directional; nasalized tokens produced in oral contexts are not "oralized". In other words, there is only one bias, and only one biasing context, and under those circumstances the basic exemplar model will result in biased variants in all contexts.

The nasalization rule, in addition to illustrating a binary process, introduces a biasing dimension other then duration. This is important because duration is significantly simpler than most phonetic variables. Additionally, duration possesses what may be a unique property: it is invariant under the transformation from production to perception (in the absence of error).[3] Thus, an architecture that can derive the correct results for phonological processes acting on duration is not guaranteed to do the same for other phonological dimensions.

Vowel nasalization seems to be quite well-understood, and to have a straightforward explanation. It arises through an inherent property of normally produced speech: coarticulation. The articulation for the nasal consonant, which involves lowering the velum so that air can flow through the nasal cavity, is initiated before the articulation of the preceding vowel is fully completed. As a result, the velum is open for some portion of the end of the vowel, meaning that nasal airflow occurs, which, by definition, means that the vowel is partially nasalized. The evolution from partial to full nasalization seems to be exactly what the basic exemplar model should account for: a gradual increase of nasalization through an iterative process in which already nasalized (biased) tokens are subject to additional nasalization (biasing) as produced tokens are converted into stored tokens, which are once again converted into production tokens. Yet we have already seen that the context-dependent version of the basic exemplar model results in a single degenerate outcome.

In fact, there is a deeper representational problem related to the source of the bias. The degree of vowel nasalization corresponds more or less directly to the extent of the vowel during which nasal airflow is present. Thus, it is a question

[3]There is, however, potential ambiguity in attributing duration differences to inherent duration, versus differences in speaking rate or prosodic contexts. See Chapter 7.

only of how early the velum is lowered. For nasalization to increase incrementally, the velum lowering must occur earlier and earlier. There is, however, no mechanism in the basic exemplar model to accomplish this. The root of the problem is the lack of an explicit production to perception mapping. That mapping will be the focus of Chapter 5. For now the focus will be on the production side, and the argument will be that, on empirical grounds, articulatory parameters cannot depend solely on the free evolution of perceptual categories. Chapter 4 will also show that explicit articulatory targets can be used to prevent the collapse and merger problem shared by Models 1–3.

4 Modeling stability & change

4.1 Contrast maintenance

In many implemented exemplar models that include production, unbounded iterative biasing is prevented via the elimination of tokens that fall in the ambiguous region between two existing categories (Wedel 2004; 2007; 2012; Blevins & Wedel 2009; Tupper 2014). If the categories are taken to be words, then discarding ambiguous tokens acts to maintain a meaning distinction that relies on a minimal sound distinction along the given phonetic dimension. The idea that sound changes which result in homophony are dispreferred in some way, has existed within historical linguistics for a long time (e.g. Martinet 1955). In recent years this notion has been revived and quantified as an inverse correlation between the probability of a sound change that neutralizes contrast x, and the number of words that are differentiated only by contrast x. This is known as the *functional load* of the contrast[1] (Surendran & Niyogi 2006; Wedel et al. 2013). In Wedel (2012), contrast maintenance (homophone avoidance) is implemented as a storage probability that is proportional to goodness of fit. Tokens that are less prototypical members of both categories have a lower probability of being retained in either category. Thus, as ambiguous tokens are lost, the two categories are effectively pushed apart. Functional load can be modeled as a weighting factor in this type of model, increasing the probability that ambiguous forms will be discarded, and effectively strengthening the contrast maintenance effect for certain words (Sóskuthy 2015).

The existence of a second contrasting category along the biasing dimension will prevent the biased category from moving past a certain point, allowing the basic exemplar models of the previous chapter to converge. The assumption of such a category, however, limits the types of sound changes that can be modeled; in particular, a sound change in which a new category is formed, presumably from the biased variants of an existing category. It is exactly this change that is adopted as the modeling gold standard in this book. Therefore, we will have to

[1]There are many other ways one might define functional load. However, it turns out that a simple minimal pair count seems to be the most useful of these.

consider what other forces can achieve stability, forces that, if general, must be included in all models, whether they are implementationally necessary or not.[2] In this chapter I will analyze, in detail, the consequences of adding production targets to the basic exemplar models of Chapter 2. In doing so I will arrive at a subset of models that meet the two criteria of boundedness and theoretical coherence. The full range of possible outcomes for this set of models will then be derived, setting the stage for an investigation of what type of architecture would be sufficient (and possibly necessary) to produce (under the appropriate conditions) the genesis of a new phoneme category.

It should be noted at this point that it is widely acknowledged that sociolinguistic factors play a central role in language change. A class of "innovators" may be required, aided by a class of "early adopters" in the actuation and spread of a change (Milroy & Milroy 1985). Change may require those with less social power to pay more attention to the speech of those with more power, leading to incorrect inferences about the source of phonetic variation (e.g. Garrett & Johnson 2013). Change may require systematic differences between individual speakers in their analysis of ambiguous data, the degree to which they compensate for phonetic biases, or some other facet of speech processing (e.g. Beddor 2009; Yu 2013). This paper does not explicitly address these aspects of sound change in that it focuses on the mental grammar of a single individual. The approach taken here, however, is not incompatible, nor inconsistent, with a theory of sound change that includes socio-indexical variables.

4.2 Articulatory targets

Many of the set of proposed universal phonological features specify articulatory parameters, such as where in the mouth the tongue tip makes contact during the production of the sound. Explicit targets of this kind are often assumed to be unnecessary in exemplar modeling, where categories are taken to be emergent – dependent only the interaction of competing forces. This assumption is aided by the practice of treating the initial distribution of tokens as arbitrary and independent of the model. A number of works have demonstrated that from a single global pressure, such as avoidance of homophony, structured categories can

[2] A goodness-of-fit function that doesn't directly reference contrast is possible in this scenario. However, it will not produce the desired effect for a single category. If prototypicality is determined by distance from the category mean, then what is acceptable will change as the mean of the category changes, which will occur because of the constant phonetic bias. Therefore, the category will move unboundedly. On the other hand, if prototypicality depends on some fixed value, then the category will not be able to shift beyond the specified limit of "goodness".

evolve (de Boer 2000; Wedel 2007; Sóskuthy 2013). However, sound categories, once established, are unlikely to be determined solely by the number of contrasts in a given language. If this were the case, then a category would be defined only by its individual members (the label /p/, for example, would be completely arbitrary, and contain no information about the use of the lips in the production of the sound). Furthermore, we would not expect the consistent phonetic differences that are found in the production of phonologically identical sounds across different languages (Keating 1985). Distributions would also be predicted to spread out on dimensions lacking a contrastive segment distinction. Although there is evidence that the absence of contrast leads to greater variation in pronunciation along that dimension (e.g. Choi 1995), this variation is not unlimited. Baker et al. (2011), for example, found a number of differences in how speakers produced American English "r" sounds. However, those differences resulted in little to no acoustic difference between productions. Despite the fact that English does not contrast different types of rhotic segments, productions do not expand to fill that large phonetic space.

4.3 Soft targets

From a purely implementational perspective, production targets offer a mechanism for avoiding unbounded shift and neutralization. Fixed targets, however, will prevent any kind of change, and render the exemplar architecture superfluous. In this section, what amounts to a semi-fixed target is adopted: a force that acts to keep tokens at a fixed location, but from which they can be perturbed to some degree by the usual biasing forces.

The semi-fixed, or "soft", duration target is expressed in (4.1), where β is a constant between 0 and 1 that determines the strength of the target, and N is the location of the target along the biasing dimension x.

(4.1) $$I(x_i) = \beta(N - x_i)$$

When the category is instantiated with a mean at N ($z = 0$), $I(x_i)$ can be conceptualized as a type of inertia, acting to keep tokens in place. The further a token moves from the target, the stronger the force pulling it back. This has the desired effect of bounding movement in either direction, while still allowing the category to shift as a whole. If I is the only force acting, then the tokens will eventually settle at the equilibrium point N, where the change in $\overline{x}$ is 0. N can also be characterized as the optimum of a function with a positive derivative when x is less than N, and a negative derivative, when x is greater than N. Regardless of the location of x, it is always being pushed in the direction of N.

The Soft Target model is built directly from the gradient context-dependent model of Section 3.2. Tokens selected randomly to occur in a biasing context are subjected to a bias that increases their value along dimension x by a small percentage (α) of their current value:

$$L(x_i) = \alpha x_i \tag{4.2}$$

Figure 4.1 shows the effect of adding a soft target to Model 2. Change is constrained relative to the basic model. This model is also theoretically interpretable; there is a single category, with a single production target corresponding to the non-biased segment, and the biasing process applies to all tokens of this category with equal probability. These properties will become important as I continue to explore the modeling space in the following sections.

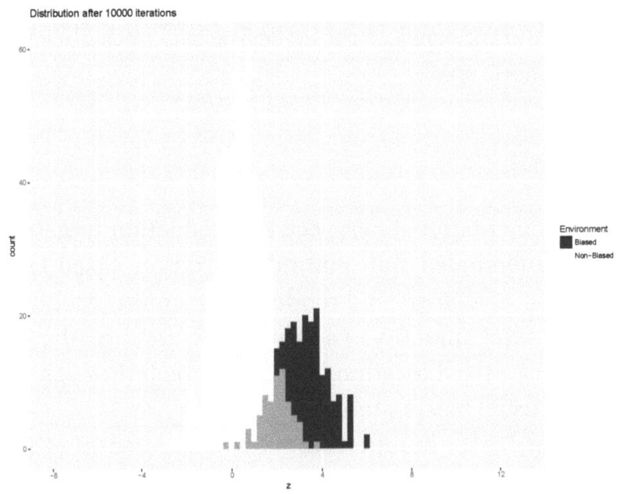

Figure 4.1: Soft-Target Model with increasing bias function. White: tokens produced in non-biasing contexts. Black: tokens produced in biasing contexts. z-normed x dimension. Observation occurs after 10,000 model cycles.

For positive x, the difference between (4.2) and (4.1) is effectively between a monotonically increasing function with an optimum at 0, and a non-monotonic function with an optimum at N. Theoretically speaking, however, the former expresses a PROCESS, while the latter expresses a STATE (cf. Hyman 1975). PROCESS will be taken to refer to what would be considered an allophonic rule in generative phonology, and to which the term "lengthening" (or "shortening") can properly apply. At the segment level (S), the general process model instantiates the following linguistic relationship: $/S/ \rightarrow [S^B]/\_B$, where B stands for the biasing context, and $[S^B]$ stands for the allophonic variant that occurs in that context. Using the same notation, a STATE model instantiates the following relationship: $/S^B/ \rightarrow [S^B]$ in context B. This indicates that S^B is stored, or underlying, rather than generated. A given STATE could consist of "long", or "lengthened", tokens but does not properly involve "lengthening".

4.4 Model space

The original lengthening model in Section 2.4.2.1 is a PROCESS model. As we saw previously, a PROCESS model that lacks a production target is unbounded, producing no stable outcomes. As will be shown in Section 4.5.2, adding a soft target to this model will result in stable outcomes for a certain range of parameter values. The analogous STATE model can be created by implementing the bias term itself as a soft target, as in (4.3) (cf. Sóskuthy 2013).

(4.3) $$L(x_i) = \alpha(L - x_i)$$

This model, with one target for non-biased tokens and one for biased tokens, can also be shown to produce stable outcomes. The no-target PROCESS model, the soft-target PROCESS model, and the STATE model, however, differ with respect to their theoretical consistency and thus linguistic interpretability.

Model 2, from Section 2.4.2.1, re-labelled as Model A in Table 4.1, is a linguistically interpretable model. There is a single category from which tokens are selected at random, either to be produced in biasing contexts, in which case they are lengthened, or to be produced in non-biasing contexts, in which case they are unchanged. Model B, with a soft target at the location of the non-biased, underlying category, is also consistent. All tokens feel a pull towards this underlying target, but those that happen to be produced in a biasing context are also subject to a force that lengthens them during production. Model C, however, the STATE model, is not theoretically consistent.

Table 4.1: Single-Category Model Space

					Stable	Consistent
A	PROCESS	$\alpha(1+x)$	No Target	–	N	Y
B	PROCESS	$\alpha(1+x)$	Target	$\beta(N-x)$	(Y)	Y
C	STATE	$\alpha(L-x)$	Target	$\beta(N-x)$	Y	N

In Model C, all tokens have a target at *N*, but tokens produced in a biasing context have an additional, conflicting target at *L*. Because there is only a single category in Model C, biased tokens are generated from the same pool as non-biased tokens, therefore the second target, *L*, exists without an underlying category with which that target can be associated. With the distribution initialized at *N*, the effect is for biased tokens to be moved an arbitrarily small distance, $\alpha(L-x)$, towards that second target during production.[3] Of the three models, only Model B is both stable (bounded) and theoretically consistent.

Model C, however, can be made theoretically consistent by introducing a second level of representations. If the parent category can be split into two sub-categories, then each target can be associated with a different sub-category. This is Model G in Table 4.2, which is the 2-level model analog of Table 4.1. The remaining models in this table are all theoretically problematic in different ways. Model D is the two sub-category counterpart of Model B. While Model B is theoretically consistent, the introduction of a separate sub-category for biased tokens in Model D creates a representational paradox: a category with no target, to which lengthening continuously applies. Model D is also unbounded. Model E re-creates the two-target paradox of Model C. Finally, F is the hybrid PROCESS+*state* model.[4]

Table 4.2: 2-Level Model Space

		biased	non-biased		Stable	Consistent
D	PROCESS	$\alpha(1+x)$	Target	$\beta(N-x)$	N	N
E	2-STATE	$\beta(N-x)$; $\alpha(L-x)$	Target	$\beta(N-x)$	Y	N
F	PROCESS+ STATE	$\alpha(1+x)$; $\alpha(L-x)$	Target	$\beta(N-x)$	Y	N
G	STATE	$\alpha(L-x)$	Target	$\beta(N-x)$	Y	Y

[3] As a PROCESS, incrementality has a straightforward interpretation: a given token is shifted, or lengthened, by a fixed proportion of its current length. But in a STATE model, in which all tokens are initialized at one target, it is not clear what mechanism would shift certain tokens only a small amount towards another target. Although, superficially, this effect is similar to that of the entrenchment force, $\varepsilon(\overline{x}-x)$, which pushes the tokens of a given category closer together, they are different in important ways. The use of the category mean in the entrenchment function stands in for the sum of the forces that act between individual tokens, maintaining category cohesion (the same effect can be achieved by averaging over multiple tokens in production, e.g. Pierrehumbert 2001; Wedel 2006). The soft target, or inertia force, on the other hand, references a fixed target location that is specified independently of the current distribution.

[4] If double specifications are possible (e.g. PROCESS + STATE), then the total set of possible models includes the Single-Category PROCESS+STATE model, and the set of non-biased No-Target models, among others. However, these other models all contain a superset of the representational inconsistencies already described, and therefore are not included.

Only two viable candidates emerge from the full set of model: a pure PROCESS model with a single target, (B), and a pure STATE model (G). In general terms, these results show us that PROCESS and STATE models are incompatible with one another. If biased tokens have a separate representational status, this implies that only tokens from this sub-category should be chosen to be produced in biased contexts. Furthermore, since the biased sub-category has a target at *L*, those tokens will already be appropriately longer than their non-biased counterparts (with a target at *N*). Therefore, there is no motivation for lengthening them further. Effectively, this would be equivalent to a phonological rule of the form:

(4.4) Process + State: $/S^B/ \rightarrow [S^{B^B}]/\_B$

Although (4.4) is linguistically ill-formed, it is equivalent to the feedback loop at the heart of the basic exemplar model.[5] Cumulativity of small differences is only possible if the bias effects in production (contextually determined allophony) are stored (STATE), rather than being stripped away during perception. Storage of allophonic detail implies that the biasing context itself is discarded, or at least not used to recover the underlying form. In production, however, the PROCESS model requires knowledge of the context that triggers biasing. In other words, the allophonic rule is available in production, but not in perception.[6]

Another way to characterize this theoretical incompatibility is that a PROCESS model implies that normalization takes place, while a STATE model implies that it does not. Thus, inconsistency results when either the production or perception stage of a given model assumes normalization, while the other doesn't. In the Pure Process Model (B), all tokens are drawn from the same distribution in production, with a target, or underlying specification, at *N*. Lengthening applies as an allophonic rule, but in perception all tokens are drawn back to the same underlying target at *N*, whether they are lengthened or not. Thus, the inertial force acts to partially normalize the effect of lengthening. Complete normalization (fixed target) would prevent change entirely. In the Pure State Model (G), on the other hand, normalization fails to occur in the sense that "lengthened" tokens are assigned to their own sub-category, and no allophonic rules apply.

[5]It should be noted that, as far as I am aware, no one has actually proposed the context-dependent exemplar models in Chapter 2. They are what I take to be the logical extension of the context-free exemplar model of Pierrehumbert (2001).

[6]The alternative is that both the unnormalized surface forms and their production context are stored, or incorporated into the category label in some way. Even if so, it is still not clear why an allophonic rule would continue to apply. Furthermore, if prior specification of complex sub-structure is required (and, in the limit, a unique category for every token), the exemplar framework does not seem to offer much, if anything, in terms of explanatory power.

Again, the STATE aspect is only partial. The fact that these are sub-categories rather than completely independent categories introduces a connection between the biased and non-biased tokens which implies that the relationship between them is known, and therefore that the allophonic transformation is known. Two entirely independent categories would preclude change entirely.

4.5 Consistent and convergent models of sound change

This section is devoted to an exhaustive analysis of the end states of the two theoretically consistent and bounded models: the Pure Process Model (B), and the Pure State Model (G). These results will be provided in the form of two parameters: the category means along the dimension x, and the difference between the means of the biased and non-biased sub-distributions. Because it is not possible to guarantee that simulations will fully sample the space of possible outcomes, stable states will be explicitly derived as a function of model parameters. The derivation will be given in abbreviated terms in the text, with the full details provided in the appendices. Following Sóskuthy (2013; 2015), the percentage of tokens produced in a biasing context (bias proportion) will act as the independent variable. The term "attractor" will also be adopted in reference to a soft target, in order to facilitate comparison to that work.

4.5.1 State Model: Sub-categories

The Pure State Model contains one target for biased tokens, and a distinct target for non-biased tokens. Figure 4.2 provides an illustration of the forces acting at some model time t, on exemplar categories modeled as normal functions. As will be shown below, the means of both sub-categories can be guaranteed to lie somewhere between the two targets at N and L. Each sub-category is subject to the inertia associated with its own target, acting to pull the two apart. Membership in a superset category is implemented via the entrenchment force, which pulls both in the direction of the global mean, and thus towards one another.[7] In this illustration, the relative number of tokens produced in biasing versus non-biasing contexts is represented by the heights of the normal curves. Because the proportion of biasing contexts is less than 50% in this example, the global mean (indicated by the dashed line) is closer to the mean of the non-biased distribution.

[7] Sóskuthy (2013) links sub-categories by applying phonetic biasing probabilistically to both, but with the biased sub-category more strongly weighted.

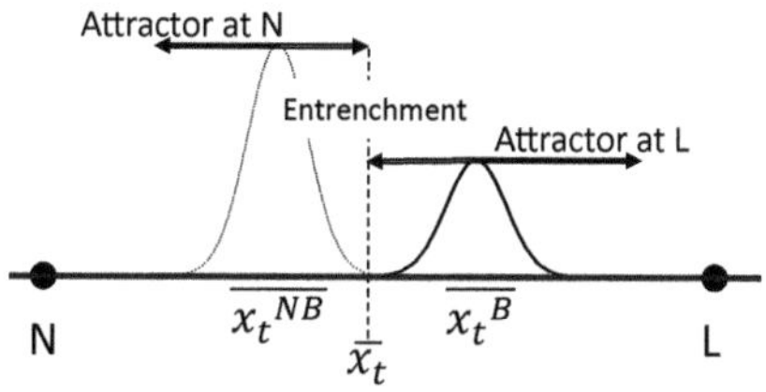

Figure 4.2: Schematic of forces for Pure State Model

The equations for each of the model forces have been given previously, but are repeated here for ease of reference: (4.5) Entrenchment, (4.6) Inertia (attractor) at *N*, and (4.7) Inertia (attractor) at *L*. A small random error term is also included in all models.

(4.5)
$$E(x_i) = \epsilon(\overline{x} - x_i)$$

(4.6)
$$I(x_i) = \beta(N - x_i)$$

(4.7)
$$L(x_i) = \alpha(L - x_i)$$

In order to estimate the behavior of this model under various conditions I will make the simplifying assumption that each sub-category is specified by a normal curve with variable mean, but fixed standard deviation. This allows us to use the mean of each sub-category as a proxy for its global behavior. To determine the stable model outputs, I use the fact that forces must balance at this equilibrium point, meaning that no further changes occur in the location of the means. Therefore, the sum of all forces is set to zero. $\overline{x_E}$ is defined as the location of the global mean at equilibrium, while $\overline{x_E^B}$ and $\overline{x_E^{NB}}$ are the equilibrium means of the biased and non-biased sub-categories, respectively.

The first step is to prove that there is no way for the mean of either sub-category (and therefore, the global mean) to have a value less than *N*, or greater than *L*. This follows from the mathematical form of the inertial, or attractor, forces. For values greater than the attractor location, the force is leftward, but for values smaller than the attractor location, the force is rightward, thus always acting to push the distribution precisely to the attractor location. If the sub-categories were completely independent (no global entrenchment), then they would always stabilize at their respective attractor locations. Entrenchment allows the sub-categories to be perturbed from their attractors, but only in the direction of the other sub-category. Thus, we can be confident that they will end up at equilibrium somewhere between N and L. The exact location will depend on the parameters α (the strength of the attractor at L), β (the strength of the attractor at N), ε (the strength of the entrenchment force), and p (the bias proportion: the percentage of the category consisting of biased tokens; in other words, the percentage of tokens produced in a biasing context).

The equilibrium location for the non-biased sub-category is determined by the point at which global entrenchment (2.1) is perfectly balanced by the attractor at N (4.1). Using the equilibrium location of the mean to stand in for the entire sub-category:

$$\beta\left(N - \overline{x_E^{NB}}\right) + \varepsilon\left(\overline{x_E} - \overline{x_E^{NB}}\right) = 0.$$

Therefore,

$$\beta\left(\overline{x_E^{NB}} - N\right) = \varepsilon\left(\overline{x_E} - \overline{x_E^{NB}}\right).$$

For the biased distribution, it is the attractor at L (4.3) that will be balanced by global entrenchment (2.1): $\alpha(\overline{x_E^B} - L) = \varepsilon(\overline{x_E} - \overline{x_E^B})$. In order to solve for the three quantities, $\overline{x_E^B}, \overline{x_E^{NB}}$, and $\overline{x_E}$, we need a third equation linking them. This is given by the equation that expresses the global mean as a weighted average of the two sub-category means.

$$\overline{x_E} = (1-p)\overline{x_E^{NB}} + p\overline{x_E^B} \tag{4.8}$$

I can now solve for each of the quantities in turn by substitution. Appendix C shows the full derivation, and demonstrates that the global mean at equilibrium, $\overline{x_E}$, can be expressed in the following terms:

$$\overline{x_E} = \frac{(1-p)\beta N(\alpha+\varepsilon) + p\alpha L(\beta+\varepsilon)}{(\beta+\varepsilon)(\alpha+\varepsilon) - (\alpha+\varepsilon)(1-p)\varepsilon - (\beta+\varepsilon)p\varepsilon} \tag{4.9}$$

as a function of the set of model parameters (α, β, N, L, p), the location of the global mean at equilibrium. The other quantity of interest is the distance between the sub-category means, which can be expressed as a function of $\overline{x_E}$:

$$\Delta\overline{x_E} \equiv \overline{x_E^B} - \overline{x_E^{NB}} = \frac{\alpha L + \varepsilon\overline{x_E}}{\alpha+\varepsilon} - \frac{\beta N + \varepsilon\overline{x_E}}{\beta+\varepsilon} \tag{4.10}$$

Keeping all other variables constant, I can now derive the behavior of these two quantities as a function of the bias proportion, p.

The change in $\overline{x_E}$ that results from a change in p is given by taking the partial derivative of Eq. (4.9). This turns out to be somewhat unwieldy to calculate in general form. In the special case when all forces have the same strength ($\alpha = \beta = \varepsilon$), I can show that Eq. (4.9) reduces to $\overline{x_E} = N + p(L - N)$. Therefore, the global category mean is a positive linear function of p, and the change in the location of that mean is constant: $\partial\overline{x_E}/\partial p = L - N$.

For other cases, it's possible to determine the general behavior of $\partial\overline{x_E}/\partial p$ even without an exact solution. Assume that the equilibrium state for a given $p = p_j$ has already been determined. Now increase p to p_k. Eq. (4.8) entails that if $p_k > p_j$ (an increase in bias proportion), then the global mean will shift closer to the biased sub-category. Because the strength of the entrenchment force depends on the distance from the global mean, this shift will, in turn, cause the entrenchment force on the non-biased sub-category to increase. Because the attractor at N and the entrenchment force are taken to be perfectly balanced at $p = p_j$, an increase in the latter will result in a shift of the non-biased sub-category toward the biased one. At the same time, the entrenchment force on the biased sub-category will decrease commensurately. In this case, a decrease in the entrenchment force causes the balance to shift in favor of the attractor at L, meaning the biased sub-category will also shift in the rightward direction. Because the sub-categories shift in the same direction, the equilibrium point for the global mean is also guaranteed to shift in that direction, and thus to increase as p increases: $\partial\overline{x_E}/\partial p > 0$.

In the special case where $\alpha = \beta = \varepsilon$, I can use the result that $\partial\overline{x_E}/\partial p = L - N$, and determine that $\partial\Delta\overline{x_E}/\partial p = 0$. Therefore, the distance between the two sub-categories remains constant in this case. The general form of the partial derivative of (4.10) with respect to p, $\partial\Delta\overline{x_E}/\partial p$, can be written as a function of the partial derivative of $\overline{x_E}$ with respect to p ($\partial\overline{x_E}/\partial p$):

(4.11) $$\frac{\partial\Delta\overline{x_E}}{\partial p} = \frac{\partial\overline{x_E}}{\partial p}\varepsilon\left[\frac{1}{\alpha+\varepsilon} - \frac{1}{\beta+\varepsilon}\right]$$

Since I know that $\partial\overline{x_E}/\partial p$ is always positive, the sign of $\partial\Delta\overline{x_E}/\partial p$ is determined by the sign of $1/(\alpha+\varepsilon) - 1/(\beta+\varepsilon)$. The sign of $1/(\alpha+\varepsilon) - 1/(\beta+\varepsilon)$ is determined by the relative sizes of the quantities $\alpha + \varepsilon$, and $\beta + \varepsilon$. Therefore, if $\alpha > \beta$ then $\partial\Delta\overline{x_E}/\partial p < 0$; and if $\alpha > \beta$, then $\partial\Delta\overline{x_E}/\partial p < 0$.

4.5.2 Process Model: Single category

The Pure Process Model contains a single category, and a single target for that category. Tokens are selected at random, with probability p, to be produced in the biasing context. This model is identical to the Soft Target Model described in Section 4.3 (Figure 4.1). It will be shown in this section that the Process Model is only stable for certain parameter values. The behavior of the global mean, and the average separation between biased and non-biased productions, will be derived as before. The same simplifying assumption that the category can be approximated as a normal distribution with fixed variance will also be made. However, it should be noted that this assumption is less justified for the one-category model due to the fact that biased and non-biased variants will separate, creating a lumpier distribution, and likely an increase in variance.

The derivational steps in this analysis are given graphically in Figure 4.3. Panel 1 is a snapshot of the model at some time, t, when the global mean is located at location $\overline{x_t}$ along x. Both biased and non-biased tokens are sampled from this distribution, at different rates. This relationship is indicated by the darker normal curve (subset of tokens subjected to bias during production) within the lighter one (subset of tokens non-biased during production).

The production value of any token at any time t can be calculated, as long as its current value, and the category mean, are known. All tokens are subject to the attractor at N. And all tokens are subject to the entrenchment force acting to pull them closer to the current category mean (which will be greater than, or equal to, N). Additionally, a proportion p of randomly selected tokens undergo a lengthening process, moving away from the rest of the distribution during production.

Panels 2–4 of Figure 4.3 take us sequentially through the application of forces. Panel 2 isolates the effect of applying the attractor and lengthening forces. The attractor affects all tokens equally, because all tokens are equally far from N on average. Lengthening, applied only to a subset of tokens, splits the distribution apart. Before entrenchment applies, the mean values for the observed productions ($\overline{x_t^B}'$, mean of biased productions in Panel 2; $\overline{x_t^{NB}}'$, mean of non-biased productions in Panel 2), can each be given as a function of the global mean at time t, $\overline{x_t}$:

(4.12)
$$\overline{x_t^B}' = \overline{x_t}(1 + \alpha) + \beta(N - \overline{x_t})$$

(4.13)
$$\overline{x_t^{NB}}' = \overline{x_t} + \beta(N - \overline{x_t})$$

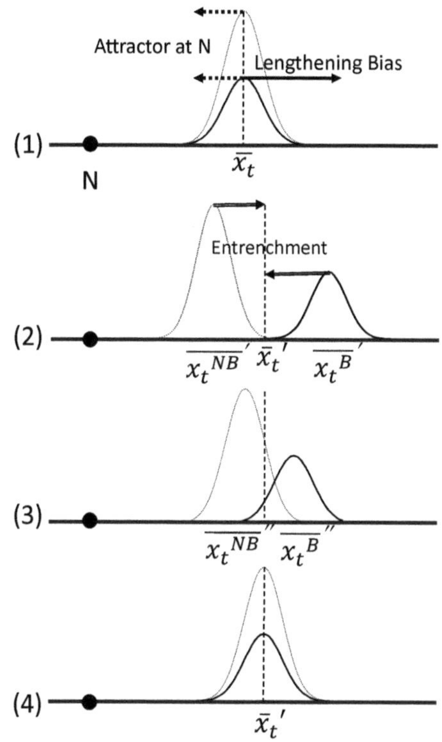

Figure 4.3: Schematic of forces for PROCESS model

Applying entrenchment does not affect the global mean, only the absolute locations of the sub-distribution means, and their separation. Therefore, the mean in Panel 3 is identical to the mean from Panel 2. This mean ($\overline{x_t}'$) is given by the weighted average of the means of the observed production variants:

$$\overline{x_t}' = (1-p)\overline{x_t^{NB}}' + p\overline{x_t^{B}}' \tag{4.14}$$

Equilibrium is achieved when continued iterations fail to change the locations of the means. This means that they should be unaffected by successive iterations of biasing. $\overline{x_E}' = \overline{x_E}$, $\overline{x^B}' = \overline{x^B}$, and $\overline{x^{NB}}' = \overline{x^{NB}}$. Therefore,

(4.15) $$\overline{x_E} = (1-p)\overline{x_E^{NB}}' + p\overline{x_E^{B}}'$$

and from Eq. (4.12) and (4.13),

(4.16) $$\overline{x_E} = (1-p)\{\overline{x_E} + \beta(N - \overline{x_E})\} + p\{\overline{x_E}(1+\alpha) + \beta(N - \overline{x_E})\}$$

Solving for $\overline{x_E}$ gives

(4.17) $$\overline{x_E} = \frac{\beta N}{\beta - p\alpha}$$

See Appendix D for the full derivation.

The behavior of the global mean as a function of p will depend on which region of parameter space we are in: $p\alpha < \beta$, or $p\alpha > \beta$. For $p\alpha < \beta$, the denominator in (4.17) is positive. Therefore, as p increases (but $p\alpha$ stays smaller than β), the denominator decreases, and the global mean increases ($\partial\overline{x_E}/\partial p > 0$). In the limit, as $p\alpha$ goes to β, the equilibrium mean goes to infinity, and lengthening is unbounded. For $p\alpha > \beta$, the denominator is negative, which also means that the mean is negative, and the only equilibrium point is negative. Since negative duration values aren't possible, there is no well-defined equilibrium in the range in which $p\alpha > \beta$. The PROCESS model is thus only stable if the lengthening strength (α) is not too great, and the percentage of biasing contexts (p) is not too large, relative to the attractor strength (β).

To calculate the second quantity of interest, the dependence of sub-distribution separation on p, the effect of entrenchment must be included. Entrenchment acts to bring all tokens back towards the global mean by an amount proportional to their distance from that mean (Panel 3 of Figure 4.3):

(4.18) $$\overline{x^B}'' = \overline{x^B}' + \varepsilon\left(\overline{x}' - \overline{x^B}'\right)$$

(4.19) $$\overline{x^{NB}}'' = \overline{x^{NB}}' + \varepsilon\left(\overline{x}' - \overline{x^{NB}}'\right)$$

The separation between the two production variants after entrenchment applies ($\Delta\overline{x}''$) can be determined by taking the difference between Equations (4.18) and (4.19):

(4.20) $$\Delta\overline{x}'' \equiv \overline{x^B}'' - \overline{x^{NB}}'' = (1-\varepsilon)\left(\overline{x^B}' - \overline{x^{NB}}'\right)$$

The final separation depends only on the separation prior to the application of entrenchment ($\Delta\overline{x}'$ in Panel 2), and the strength of the entrenchment term, ε. Because the sub-distributions only exist at production, no cumulativity in separation is possible (see Panel 4). Therefore, at all times t, the separation in Panel 2, prior to entrenchment, will always be given by the lengthening factor: $\alpha\overline{x_t}$. Therefore, at equilibrium, when $\overline{x_t} = \overline{x_E}$, the average distance between the two production sub-distributions is given by

$$\Delta\overline{x_E} = (1 - \epsilon)(\alpha\overline{x_E}). \tag{4.21}$$

In the stable parameter range ($p\alpha > \beta$), where $\overline{x_E}$ increases as p increases, the separation of the sub-distributions also increases, but more slowly, by a factor of $(1 - \epsilon)\alpha$.

4.6 Change between stable states

Most work in the exemplar framework models either change or stability, but not both. That is to say, only one stable state is possible, and the model either starts in that state, in which case it remains there for all time, or inevitably arrives in that state from any other starting conditions. In Garrett & Johnson (2013) there are two different modes of processing,[8] resulting in essentially two different models: one in which normalization occurs, which is stable, and one in which normalization is "turned off", leading to change (the latter model is not implemented, but would lead to unbounded shift without an additional mechanism). Kirby (2014) is similar in that two different outcomes are possible, one for a "misparsing" mode, and one for accurate parsing (in the "misparsing" mode, merger is prevented by a stage of hypothesis selection in which a Bayesian learner updates phonetic cue weights so as to optimize categorization accuracy).

"Agent-based" models (not all implemented using exemplar representations) use the interaction among one or more groups of speakers to be the driving mechanism, either of the evolution of language itself, or of the evolution of pre-existing variants (which may be parameters, or entire grammars). Systems are taken to be stable within individual speakers, that is, without bias. Thus there is no mechanism via which a truly novel form can arise, only ways in which an existing distribution can evolve within a heterogeneous population (Niyogi &

[8]These are likened to "speech" and "non-speech" processing modes (Liberman et al. 1967); individual speakers may switch between the two modes, or different speakers may operate consistently in one or the other mode (e.g. Yu 2013).

Berwick 1997; de Boer 2000; Nowak et al. 2001; Steels 2005; Baxter et al. 2006; Oudeyer 2006; Fagyal et al. 2010; Stanford & Kenny 2013; Pierrehumbert et al. 2014). Models that rely on simple "self-organizing" principles, such as random selection, or mis-classification, are usually designed to demonstrate that a single optimal state will be reached from any starting position (Wedel 2006; Ettlinger 2007; Wedel 2007; Blevins & Wedel 2009; Tupper 2014; Wedel & Fatkullin 2017). Some additional mechanism would be needed to change such systems further. Effectively, actuation is achieved either through speaker contact (in which adoption of already existing variants may occur), or by initializing the model in an unstable state.

As far as I am aware, Sóskuthy (2013) and Sóskuthy (2015) are unique in the literature in that they capture both change and stability within a single model. Actuation occurs via a completely speaker-internal mechanism that is an integral component of the model: allophone frequency. Model 1 in Section 2.4.1 was an instantiation of frequency of use as an instigator of change, in the successive reduction of highly frequent words. In that model, frequency was a fixed property of a given word type. But changes in word frequency, as well as in the relative proportion of contextual variants, are possible for independent reasons. Words go in and out of style, and the frequency of use of any given word is expected to change over time. In turn, changes in frequency at the word level also affect the frequency of occurrence of the phonemes that make up the word. A change in allophone frequency could also result if the words affected happened to contain the same allophonic environment.

The model of vowel lengthening in Sóskuthy (2013) was the basis for the gradient context-dependent model first introduced in Section 2.4.2. This model was gradually developed, first into a set of possible models implementing at least one soft target, then into a subset of those that were both stable and theoretically consistent. The remaining two models were then implemented with frequency of allophonic environment (bias proportion) as the actuator of change. Sóskuthy (2013) is actually closest to Model E (Section 4.4), as a two-target STATE model. The vowel-level category is modeled as a mixture of Gaussians, namely the subcategory of variants that occur in the lengthening context and the sub-category of variants that occur in the non-lengthening context. Instead of global entrenchment, the link to the superset category is implemented by applying lengthening stochastically to tokens chosen from both sub-categories, but with the "long" subcategory more strongly weighted. Additionally, a "centering bias", implemented as an attractor at *N*, is used to prevent unbounded dispersion.[9] The mathemati-

[9]This is necessary to counteract the contrast maintenance pressure that pushes categories away from one another, via elimination of ambiguous tokens (Wedel 2012 and Blevins & Wedel 2009).

cal form of the attractor function is equivalent to the soft target first introduced in Section 4.3: an inertial force that applies when tokens are perturbed from an underlyingly specified position, acting to pull them back towards that position. This results, functionally, in two targets for the biased sub-category (one at N and one at L).[10]

Sóskuthy's model therefore differs from the Pure State Model implemented in Section 4.5.1. The actual model behavior, however, turns out to be quite similar. As we saw in the previous section, changes in bias proportion – how often the biasing context occurs relative to the non-biasing context – act to shift the model from one stable state to another. The global mean of the vowel category always increases with increasing p, but the separation between the "lengthened" and "unlengthened" variants can increase, decrease, or stay the same, depending on other model parameters.[11] Under the assumption that parameter values are fixed for a given speaker, only one of those outcomes will actually be possible for each individual.

4.7 Phoneme split

Existing exemplar models of change are actually models of phonetic, rather than phonological, change. The framework offers the possibility that low-level synchronic variation, like phonetic nasalization, can successively accumulate, leading to large-scale change. However, the basic framework does not, in and of itself, offer a solution to the actuation problem at the phonological level. We know that new phonological categories can form over time, and this seems to happen when phonetic allophones achieve independence from their parent categories. Thus, the outcome in which lengthened vowels become contrastive long vowels, and nasalized vowels become contrastive nasal vowels, is of particular interest. It has been proposed that phoneme genesis is triggered by a subset of phonetic variants that have shifted sufficiently far from the rest of the distribution (Janda & Joseph 2003; Janda 2008). This is essentially what is assumed in Wedel (2012), with phonemic contrast equated to the emergence of a bi-modal distribution. However, as we saw in the STATE model of Section 4.5.1, "long" tokens can never get longer than their attractor at L, and the distance between

[10] Sóskuthy (2015) employs a similar architecture. There is an explicit target for only the biased sub-category, but all tokens are affected by the same centering force. In this model, hard thresholds at 0 and 1 act to force both distributions back towards the center, similarly to how a target attracts tokens from either direction. These attractors are critical to achieving stable states in both models.

[11] In Sóskuthy's models there is a somewhat more complex dependence on p.

the two sub-categories is similarly constrained by the distance between the two attractors. This is problematic if phonetic exaggeration or "enhancement" is necessary to initiate a new phonological category. The PROCESS model seems to offer more potential for phonological change if lengthening can be somehow turned off right after biased tokens achieve sufficient separation from the non-biased part of the distribution. In fact, what is needed to model phoneme split with the current set of models is precisely a mechanism that will enact the necessary representational changes needed to convert a PROCESS model (allophony) to a STATE model (contrast).[12]

In addition to the question of how the transition from PROCESS to STATE can occur, there is the separate question of the level at which the STATE is specified. Features, such as [*voice*], or [*nasal*], are usually considered to be the universal atoms from which all phonemes are constructed. However, a given rule, or process, acts over some set of phonemes within a given language. Each individual phoneme consists of a unique matrix of feature values, but the phoneme class is specified by the subset of feature values that all members share (comprising a natural class). In principle, any combination of feature values for any subset of features could be a natural class that is linguistically relevant in some language. Yet the number of such classes that are actually used, or active, within a given language is much smaller. Furthermore, the existence, or activity, of a particular natural class within a language is identified only by the fact that all and only the phonemes that belong to that class behave identically with respect to some rule. It is uncontroversial that the rule must be learned by the speaker of the language, and therefore, which natural class is associated with the rule must also be learned. Thus, it is not unlikely that the natural class itself is learned, or formed, at the time the rule is learned. This view is further supported by the possible existence of "unnatural" classes (e.g. Mielke 2008).

[12]Going from a STATE to a PROCESS model, on the other hand, requires that independent categories become linked through the inference of a predictable relationship between them. In one sense, phoneme merger is clearly the opposite of phoneme split in that the former reduces the number of independent categories, while the latter increases them. However, phoneme merger is not equivalent to (re-)establishing an allophonic relationship. As far as I am aware, merger is taken to be the result of phonetic overlap among distinct categories (that may or may not share allophones) involving the wholesale replacement of one category with another occupying the exact same phonetic space. A change from a STATE to a PROCESS, therefore, may be a different kind of change, and perhaps one that has no exact correspondent in the standard taxonomy of sound change. This is an intriguing avenue for future work.

In the case of vowel lengthening, the relevant class of segments that undergo the rule consists of the natural class that specifies all and only vowels. The class of segments that act as the trigger, or environment, for the rule is the set of all non-continuant non-nasal voiced segments. In both the STATE and PROCESS models this sub-category is explicitly represented, and in fact, the models are initialized with this representation.[13] This assumption begs the sound change question to a large extent. If there was a prior period in which no rule of vowel lengthening existed, then the more interesting question might be where it came from in the first place? In other words, how did precisely this natural class, this sub-category of phonological units, become linguistically active in this language. Because this is the starting point for these models, however, there is no mechanism for generating new allophonic relationships, or for eliminating them altogether.[14]

How abstract categories are formed in the first place, how many, with what kinds of sub-structures, are questions that are far from being definitively answered (see, among others, Peperkamp et al. 2006; Dillon et al. 2013; Feldman et al. 2009; McMurray & Jongman 2011; Goldsmith & Xanthos 2009). It is reasonable to expect that greater knowledge of how categories are formed will lead to greater insight into how sound changes occur, and what kinds of sound changes are possible. It is beyond the scope of this paper to propose a general theory of category formation. However, in the next chapter, I will explore some models in which the basic units to which forces apply are distinct from the featural description of the linguistic phenomenon. In Chapters 5 and 6 I will also modify, or replace, many of the assumptions explicitly laid out in Chapters 1–4, including the very definition of phoneme split.

[13]It is worth noting that [*vowels before everything else*] does not actually comprise a natural class due to its disjoint nature, consisting of the union of the following natural classes: [*vowels before continuants*], [*vowels before nasals*], and [*vowels before voiceless non-continuants*]. In descriptions of the phenomenon, the comparison class is typically non-continuants that are voiceless, and this is likely to be assumed as the relevant second sub-category for modeling purposes.

[14]Treating sub-categorization as a phonetic, rather than a phonemic, distinction does not solve this problem if the necessary structure is still stipulated, and the prior existence of the allophonic rule is assumed (e.g. Dillon et al. 2013).

5 The relationship between perception and production

In the models examined to this point, the tokens of perception have been assumed to be identical to the tokens of production. This assumption obscures the fact that targets in production are necessary in order for sounds to be produced at all, i.e., that read-out of a stored set of acoustic values is not possible. It also conflates biases that act in production with those that act in perception, requiring them to act on the same units. Furthermore, this assumption requires that complex articulatory dynamics be uniquely and transparently realized acoustically. For a dimension like segment duration, this assumption may not be too unreasonable. However, the correspondence between articulation and acoustics is well known to be a many-to-many mapping. Invariant cues to abstract phonemes have failed to be discovered in either domain.

Starting at least with Goldinger (1996), it has been assumed that experienced exemplars are stored as motor plans without intermediate processing. While this may be adopted largely as an implementational convenience, it is based on the assumption that the true details of the mapping will not significantly affect the mechanism of change, or the model outcomes (see Pierrehumbert 2001). Perhaps the most critical assumption is that they will not affect the feedback loop that is the driving mechanism of such models. However, as this chapter will demonstrate, a non-trivial perception-to-production mapping is not just an additive factor that can be slotted into existing models, but a shift in perspective that affects all aspects of modeling, up to and including what we take to be the source of sound change itself. The following sections will make these ramifications explicit for three cases representing three different types of phonetic bias (two of which have been previously modeled): vowel lengthening (duration-based targets); vowel nasalization (sequencing of different articulators); and velar palatalization (sequencing of different targets for the same articulator).

5.1 Duration-based targets

The lack of motivation for a process by which a production, at some random point along the relevant dimension, is moved only a small amount towards its target, was mentioned briefly in Section 4.4. Failure to completely achieve a target may not seem paradoxical at first glance, because it suggests a well-known articulatory phenomenon, known as "undershoot", in which targets fail to be completely achieved (e.g. Lindblom 1963). But this is not an equivalent process.[1]

Undershoot can occur if over-all speech rate is rapid, not allowing enough time to overcome the inertia inherent in the physical articulators, or if sequential targets involving the same articulator (e.g. tongue body) are far apart in the mouth. A duration target, however, cannot be undershot in the same way. In the first place, segment duration *per se* is not specified on individual articulators or their configurations. Furthermore, duration is not absolute. Thus, although a faster speaking rate will lead to shorter vowel durations, it will also shorten all segments in all contexts, meaning that the relative difference between vowel durations in pre-voiced versus pre-voiceless contexts will not necessarily be affected (unless duration values are at floor or ceiling). A speaking rate transformation effectively changes the location of the target itself in absolute terms; it does not affect the speaker's ability to reach that target for any given token. Length-based features are arguably better modeled by targets that are a function of speaking rate.

With respect to the effect of frequency on duration, the mechanism, and its interaction with speaking rate, remains somewhat unclear. In models of frequency effects, speaking rate does not seem to be considered. Yet the parallels between the two are clear. The conceptualization of frequency of use as repeated practice suggests that there exists a maximally fluent, or optimal, production target. While increased frequency should not reduce any word below that target, increased speaking rate might. If frequency of use translates to higher resting activation, on the other hand, and higher resting activation leads to faster production, successive shortening should only occur if listeners fail to normalize for speaking

[1]The centering bias in Wedel (2012) is characterized as a lenition bias towards the center of each segment dimension. Because Wedel's categories lack underlying targets (they are randomly generated and evolve as poor, or ambiguous, tokens are discarded), his lenition bias is the mechanism that prevents categories from dispersing indefinitely. For a two-dimensional phonetic vowel space composed of the first and second formant frequencies, a centralizing bias is fairly consistent with undershoot. However, this bias is implemented as a fixed attractor location, rather than a process that shifts the vowel formants a small amount towards the center of formant space on each production. This suggests that there is a target, or ideal, vowel location from which all vowels are perturbed by other forces.

rate; and if they fail to normalize for speaking rate, then the stored distribution will reflect the typical variance in speaking rate. This issue will be taken up in Chapter 6, with two different implementations of the frequency effect.

5.2 Coordination of independent articulators

In the vowel nasalization example of Section 3.3 it was assumed that nasalization occurred when a given vowel token was produced adjacent to a nasal consonant, transforming from completely oral ([−*nasal*]), to completely nasal ([+*nasal*]). This simulation was useful for illustrating the context mismatch that would result from nasalized tokens being produced in a non-nasal context (which occurs whether nasality is considered binary or not). Our current purpose, however, is to consider how an articulatory phenomenon like nasality could be modeled iteratively with the classic perception-production loop.

In most exemplar models "phonetic bias" is taken to apply without limit, and without regard to input values. That is, lengthening will occur regardless of how long the vowel already is, provided it occurs in a pre-voiced context. For the phenomenon of vowel nasalization this requires some partial nasalization that applies whenever a vowel is produced preceding a nasal consonant, a partial nasalization that is additive in nature. This is schematized in (5.1).

(5.1) $Nasalization(V) \rightarrow V^{+N}$
$Nasalization(V^{+N}) \rightarrow V^{+2N}$
$Nasalization(V^{+2N}) \rightarrow V^{+3N}$

But this type of acoustic cumulativity is only possible under a very specific, and unlikely, production model.

As first described in Section 3.3, phonetic vowel nasalization is the product of the coarticulation that occurs throughout normal speech. Sounds are not produced in strict sequence but overlap considerably with their neighbors. In the case of a vowel-nasal sequence, the velum, or soft palate, is raised in anticipation of the nasal segment before the vowel gesture has completed, resulting in airflow through the nasal cavity during at least part of the vowel's production. To represent the articulatory side of this phenomenon, and draw a clear distinction between perceived tokens and their correspondents in production, I will make use of the representational tools of Articulatory Phonology (AP) (Ohala et al. 1986; Browman & Goldstein 1990).

In AP, the abstract representational units of speech are taken to be analogous to musical scores, which indicate the coordination and ordering of a series of physical movements (articulatory gestures). Those gestures involve a set of active articulators – the tongue, velum, glottis, etc. – usually in relation to a set of passive articulator locations – the teeth, lips, hard palate, etc. Scores consist of a series of target locations for each active articulator (e.g. the alveolar ridge behind the teeth), and timing relations between those movements (e.g. begin movement of tongue tip at midpoint of open glottis gesture). Figure 5.1a depicts a gestural score for nasal coarticulation, based on the specific sequence /æm/. Time is represented along the x-axis, and the active articulators are shown on the y-axis (TB = Tongue Body; VEL = velum). The box adjacent to each active articulator represents the time span during which that articulator is activated: gradually moving towards it target position, then away to a subsequent target, or resting state. The interval during wh … :he two articulators are active a …)ace between the dotted lines … ition of interest.

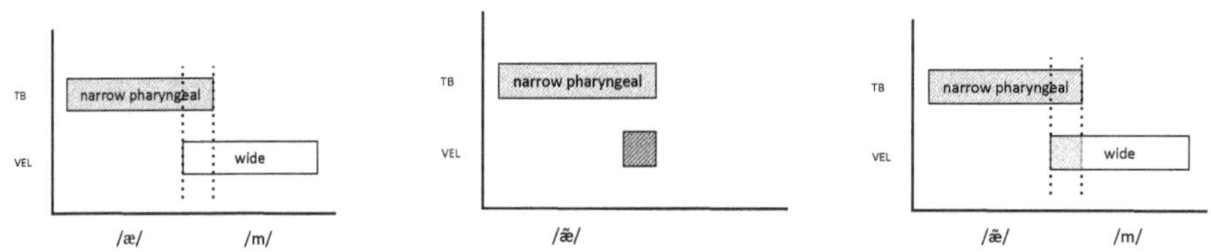

(a) Nasalization of under lyingly oral vowel token

(b) Underlyingly nasalized vowel token (unnormalized)

(c) Nasalization of underlyingly nasal vowel token

Figure 5.1: Coarticulation involving different articulators

The gestural score indicated in Figure 5.1a produces the acoustic realization [æ̃m]. The vocalic portion of this token, if stored without normalization, is represented by /æ̃/. The two different types of brackets are used here in exactly their usual sense: square brackets indicate a surface form, an instance of speech, while forward slashes indicate an underlying form, a form used to generate a speech act. Before such an acoustic token can be produced, however, it must be converted to an articulatory representation. This is shown in Figure 5.1b. Note that, despite the fact that the nasalization is now a property of the vowel itself, the same two articulatory gestures are still required in production.

At some still later model cycle, when the token represented in Figure 5.1b is chosen for production in the identical nasal context, the combined articulatory score is realized as Figure 5.1c. Under error-free perception and production, the velum gesture associated with the vowel (indicated by diagonal fill lines), and the velum gesture associated with the nasal will overlap completely. And because there is only one velum, there will be only one velum gesture. Acoustically, this will result in exactly the same amount of nasality on the vowel as before ([æ̃]). The feedback loop is, in fact, halted after a single iteration. The only way that the vowel could become successively more nasalized is if the velum were to begin raising earlier and earlier in time – in other words, if a successive change in the timing relationship were to occur.[2] But a change of this nature requires independent motivation. In other words, the iterative result does not come for free when the acoustic-articulatory mapping is no longer an identity relation.

5.3 Competing targets for the same articulator

The final case of perception-to-production mapping considered here is one that contains conflicting consecutive specifications for a single articulator. A common phenomenon of this type is palatalization, which involves the tongue shifting towards the hard palate (either forward or backward) due to the influence of a following or preceding segment (Guion 1998; Keating & Lahiri 1993). Palatalization often occurs in sequences of obstruent consonants and high vowels. For example, in the articulation of the sequence /ki/, the articulatory target of the /k/ is the velum, or soft palate, where the tongue body makes contact, briefly creating a complete closure in the oral cavity. The articulatory target for the vowel is closer to the hard palate, where the tongue body should reach its highest point, but without making contact. As a result of the upcoming tongue body specification for the /i/, the tongue position for the /k/ is shifted forwards – away from the soft palate, and towards the hard palate. The result is a "blend", something that is in between where the two gestures would be in isolation (Ohala et al. 1986; Zsiga 2000).

The blended production for the palatalized velar is depicted in Figure 5.2a. At the bottom of the figure, the boxes represent temporal extent as before, this time of the single Tongue Body articulator. Diagonal fill lines represent the duration when the /k/ target is active, and the semi-opaque white, the duration of the active /i/ articulation. Above, the trajectory of the highest point of the tongue body relative to the two target locations is indicated by the dotted line. The

[2] Differences in the amount of velar opening and degree of velar airflow can be found among different types of nasalized vowels (Bell-Berti 1993; Hajek & Maeda 2000). But this is a property of a given vowel. There is no reason for the greater degree of velar opening for a low vowel, for example, to be increased further each time that vowel is produced preceding a nasal.

tongue body is assumed to start from a resting position that places its highest point somewhere in between the hard and soft palates. With the start of the /k/ gesture, movement of the tongue body is initiated towards the soft palate. However, because the gesture of the following /i/ is anticipated, a shift in direction takes place before this target is reached, causing both targets to be only partially achieved (the solid curves indicate the target trajectories for each segment in isolation).

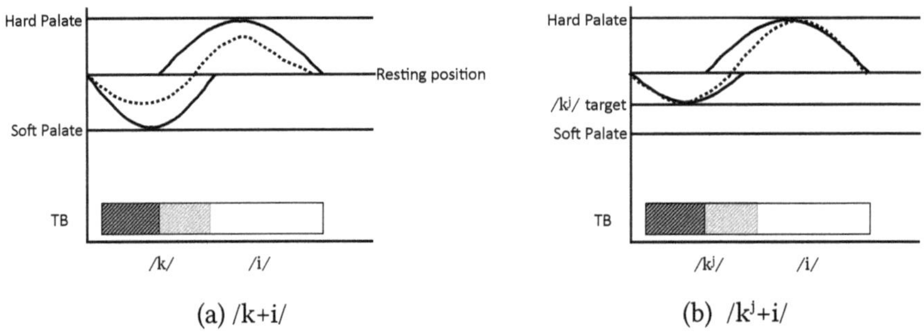

Figure 5.2: Coarticulation involving the same articulator. The dark solid lines represent the trajectories of each segment in isolation. The dotted line represents the actual trajectory. The Tongue Body (TB) is taken to start and finish in a resting position in between the two targets.

I will take the acoustic counterpart to this production token to correspond to a sequence of partially palatalized velar and high front vowel, [kʲ], [i]. The articulatory representation associated with the acoustic representation /kʲ/ contains a TB gesture located at the minimum of the dotted curve in Figure 5.2a. On a subsequent production cycle in which this token is produced in the context of a following /i/ (/kʲ+i/), the "palatalizing bias" will result in something like the dotted curve in Figure 5.2b. Effectively, the strength of the bias has been reduced. This is because the amount of bias depends on the distance between the two targets, and the target of the /kʲ/ is closer to the target of the /i/. In fact, it may now be possible to reach both targets via a slight modification in the gestural timing. In other words, there is no clear necessity of (continuously) shifting the target location for the obstruent closer to the hard palate, resulting in successively more palatalized tokens.

There is actually more than one plausible acoustic interpretation of the output of Figure 5.2a, and thus more than one articulatory mapping for tokens derived from the original production of the /k+i/ sequence. The target locations of both the consonant and the vowel may be altered, or the perceived boundary between the two segments may be shifted, or both. Figure 5.3 depicts a scenario in which the entire sequence has been stored as an exemplar of the original /k/ category: a composite segment consisting of two sequenced targets.[3] This particular type of mapping is of considerable interest because it is not structure-preserving at the phoneme level. If the perception-to-production mapping itself is the cause of the loss or the gain o[...]ut an independent chan[...]ollow directly from a me[...]

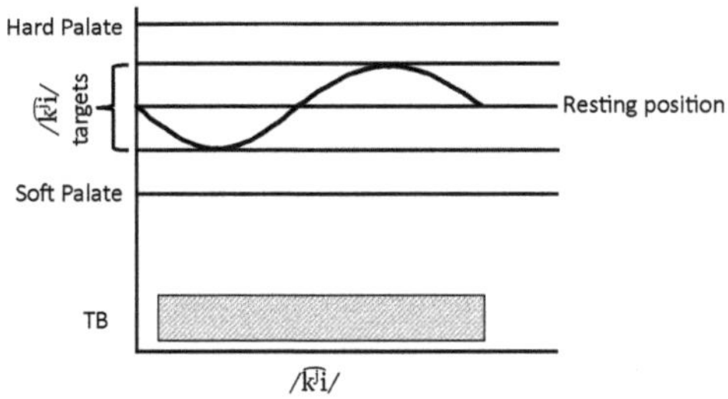

Figure 5.3: Possible production token derived from perception token [kʲi]

5.4 Misperception & misarticulation

A well-established tradition in laboratory phonology attributes phonetic and phonological sound change to mishearing and misspeaking on the part of individual speakers and listeners (Ohala 1981a,b; 1983; 1990). Many such changes are traced to coarticulation in production, which can create perceptual ambiguity, and the possibility that what the listener recovers is not what the speaker intended. In certain theories of change, the rarity of sound change is attributed to the fact that most speech takes place in a mode where speakers provide sufficient cues for listeners, and listeners accurately reverse the effects of coarticulation. Only rarely do listeners switch to a "non-speech" mode, in which they take the perceived forms at face value, or randomly decide to keep a poor category exemplar, rather than discard it (e.g. Lindblom 1990; Garrett & Johnson 2013). In other theories, discrepancies between speaker and listener are more common, and the rarity of language-wide change is attributed to the listener's access to other sources of information about the "correct" form of a word (and/or the low

[3]Using the IPA to represent acoustic correspondents is not ideal, due not only to the conflation of acoustic and articulatory information, but because it is not fine-grained enough to capture all the relevant differences among the gestural scores. The composite analysis could alternatively be represented as /kʲ/ (as opposed to the original /kʲ/+/i/). A change in both targets might look like /kʲ/+/ɪ/. Other possibilities include: /k/+/j/+/i/, /k/+/j/, /k͡j/.

likelihood of other speakers adopting and spreading an individual's novel variant, e.g. Ohala 1981a).

Perception biases emerge when segment *x* is more likely to be misheard as segment *y*, than segment *y* to be misheard as segment *x*. Production biases, in some cases, can be attributed to the masking of overlapping articulatory gestures in rapid or casual speech. These biases are of the same kind as those adopted in the preceding models. Yet a fundamental aspect of the nature of these misanalyses has been lost in implementation. Even in models that explicitly invoke the Evolutionary Phonology framework (see Blevins 2004), the mechanism is typically realized at a very coarse grain.[4] For example, the model in Wedel & Fatkullin (2017) (also described in Blevins & Wedel 2009) is driven by misperception error (or "variant trading"); this occurs as a binary decision between neighboring lexical categories. As already discussed, Garrett & Johnson (2013) implement an all-or-nothing normalization mechanism.[5] In Kirby (2014), "misparsing" is more gradient; for any given token, a random amount of the target segment may be mis-attributed to the preceding segment. However, the misparsing doesn't depend on the phonetic properties of the input, and different outcomes are only possible by "turning off" the misparsing. Morley (2014) uses a bi-directional misperception term in a model of velar palatalization, but misperception only applies to feature parsing, and is segment preserving.

In the next chapter a new model of vowel nasalization is developed, guided by the goal of avoiding the theoretical and implementational pitfalls laid out in this, and preceding, chapters. This model will contain an explicit listener analysis stage in which each token is parsed into its constituent units and the number of possible units is not fixed. Neither misparsing nor multiple processing modes is required because the input is not assumed to come pre-segmented at the phoneme level. Therefore, surface variation is directly reflected in underlying variation and change in one leads to change in the other.

[4]Although de Boer (2000) uses a non-trivial mapping from acoustic data to production targets, it is not a model of sound change, but of structure emergence in vowel systems. In a similar type of model, Oudeyer (2006) relies on the same units (neurons) being used in perception and production. However, this mapping is mediated by the distributed nature of the representations (over a network of neurons), and the fact that neurons are "tuned" by experienced input, via a non-linear activation function.

[5]Although they make an explicit distinction between a word-level perceptual token space, and a segment-level production token space, no transformation algorithm is provided. They also suggest that the articulatory "speech" mode is sometimes available for perception, so the exact relationship between the two "modes" of processing is somewhat unclear. In practice, the models seem to be implemented using a single abstract phonetic dimension.

6 Phoneme split

In this chapter I will develop a model of phoneme split, or genesis, using the phenomenon of vowel nasalization as a case study. The model will be based on the analyses of the preceding chapters: the metric of success will be representational consistency and stability, with the ability to achieve multiple stable states under different parameter settings. The relevant parameters will also be required to serve as testable hypotheses about possible actuation mechanisms. The first of two model variants, the No-Phoneme Model, will contain explicit representations only at the word level, and will be used primarily to illustrate a particular implementation of the frequency effect. The subsequent model, the Multiple-Parse Model, will add a sub-lexical level of analysis. The major innovation of this model will be an explicit, non-one-to-one, perception-to-production mapping in which the likelihood of a given analysis depends on the phonetic properties of the input. Additionally, no analysis is taken to be more "correct" than any other, just as the set of possible sub-lexical units is not taken to be determined ahead of time.

6.1 Representations I

It has been well-established in both perception and production that there is a negative correlation between degree of vowel nasalization and strength of nasal consonant (e.g. Kawasaki 1978; Cohn 1990). This is consistent with the hypothesis that the final nasal is more likely to be lost, the more nasalized the preceding vowel becomes. A possible explanation can be found in a listener-oriented theory of change, where speakers strive to preserve acoustic cues for ease of listener comprehension. Strong nasal cues on the vowel predict the upcoming nasal, which means that speakers may expend less effort to preserve the actual nasal, allowing it to erode. As with other proposals, the question that still remains to be answered is how the vowel came to have such strong nasal cues in the first place (presumably stronger than the typical range of phonetic nasalization observed cross-linguistically).

A different perspective will be adopted here, building on the observation of Beddor (2009) that the negative correlation between vowel nasality and consonant nasality follows directly from a single articulatory parameter: the degree of overlap of the vowel and nasal gestures. The more overlap, the greater the extent of nasalization on the vowel, and the shorter the duration of the purely consonantal nasal, and vice versa (see Figure 5.1a). It will be assumed that successful production requires stored articulatory targets, and that these must be inferred from acoustic inputs. For simplicity, only a single word type will be modeled, that consisting of a tongue body gesture followed by a velum gesture (e.g. *am*). The production-perception mapping will take place over three phonetic variables: duration of tongue body gesture, duration of velum gesture, and duration of gestural overlap (x^V, x^N, x^O). Categorization will occur at the level of the word, and does not require decomposition into phonemes. Thus, these models will not assume that there exists an allophonic process of vowel nasalization. The initial distributions for all tokens will be generated by independent sampling from three separate normal distributions, corresponding to x^V, x^N, and x^O, respectively.

In Chapter 4 we saw that (soft) targets were needed to constrain the basic exemplar model of change. What this did was effectively force an independent production component into a model which otherwise equated acoustic and articulatory representations. In the current set of models this is not necessary, implementationally, or conceptually, because each acoustic token has its own production target. This is depicted schematically in Figure 6.1, where stored articulatory parameters (represented by temporally overlapping articulatory gestures) are realized as acoustic tokens during production (dark patterned rectangles representing sound frequency information over time), and acoustic tokens are, in their turn, transformed into stored articulatory parameters during perception. At the word level, this is a STATE model; the articulatory variables are stored without normalization. At the gestural level, however, there is the possibility of an implicit PROCESS model in the fact that the overlap dimension represents the concatenation of two units, as well as the source of nasalization. I will return to this point below.

As Section 4.5 showed, the two-attractor (STATE model) had a limited range of output states: the entire distribution always stabilizes at some point intermediate between the two attractors. Furthermore, that model contained no mechanism for changing the attractor locations, or introducing new attractors. The current model effectively explodes the number of attractors (or underlying representations) to the number of tokens within a category. This allows for more complex model dynamics. It also allows for changes to occur to the attractors themselves, via independent forces that act, not at the level of the word (or at the level of the phoneme), but at the level of the gestural variables. Individual tokens of a given word category can thus be altered, with the possibility, but not the guarantee, that such changes can spread throughout the entire distribution of tokens.

V I

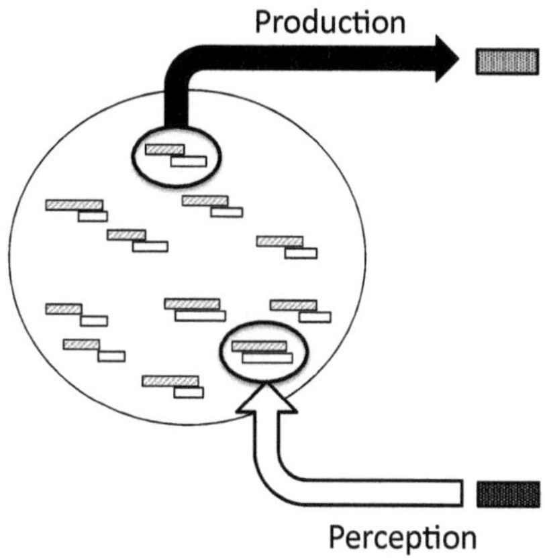

Figure 6.1: Graphical depiction of an explicit mapping between articulatory representations and acoustic representations

6.2 Frequency I

The first iteration of the phoneme-split model uses a frequency-based attractor as the actuator of change. Based on the assumption that frequency-based reduction is the result of increased fluency, and that to be fluent is to produce some (nearly) ideal balance of efficiency and intelligibility, an optimal degree of gestural overlap, *T*, is defined. Relative word frequency is implemented as a parameter (β; $0 < \beta < 1$) that controls the degree to which each token of the category is shifted towards the target, *T*, during production. Thus, for a stored production token consisting of the duration triple (x_i^V, x_i^N, x_i^O), a fluency effect applies to the ultimate realization of x_i^O, the gestural overlap value, in the following way:

(6.1) $$Fluency : x_i^{O'} = x_i^O + \beta(T - x_i^O)$$

Because the absolute duration of the optimal gestural overlap will depend on the durations of the gestures for each specific token, T is expressed as a function of x_i^N. In the case where $T = x_i^N$, the fluency pressure always acts to increase x_i^O (as long as $x_i^O \neq x_i^N$), because the duration of overlap can never be larger than the duration of the nasal gesture (assuming also that x_i^V is always greater than x_i^N).

6.3 Speaking rate

As has already been demonstrated several times, a single attractor results in a single possible outcome. With only the frequency attractor acting on productions, maximal fluency is the only possible outcome, regardless of the value of β. Implementationally, a force is needed to counter-act the fluency effect. For a fluency target at maximal overlap, that opposing force must act to decrease overlap. However, in the general case, it may be desirable to include a force that can either increase or decrease the relevant parameter values. In fact, regardless of the implementational requirements for a successful model, there are clear theoretical reasons to include a bi-directional force affecting articulatory durations.

Changes in speaking rate, of course, strongly influence the absolute duration of speech sounds. Furthermore, there are similarities between the reduction effects observed in fast speech, and those observed with high-frequency words. Therefore, whatever drives changes in speaking rate is clearly relevant in a model of change in which duration plays a role. Equally important is the fact that changes in speaking rate are not all increases in speed, and the effect of slowed speech in potentially disrupting cumulative change cannot be selectively ignored.

Changes in speaking rate have been shown to affect both the absolute duration as well as the timing between sequential speech units (Stetson 1928; Hardcastle 1985), and therefore are taken to affect all of (x^V, x^N, x^O) in the phoneme-split model. I will adopt the view here that changes in speaking rate are governed by forces largely external to the mechanisms of sound change, and that changes in rate can therefore be modeled as a stochastic process.[1]

Changes in speaking rate, affecting word duration, are modeled in the following way. At production, a value is randomly selected from a normal distribution centered about 0. This value represents the force (E) that will act on that token: either to expand it (if positive), or to compress it (if negative). Expansion results in longer words, corresponding to slower speaking rates, and compression results in shorter words, corresponding to faster speaking rates. Each articulatory parameter is independently subjected to this force. The degree to which a given gesture is actually expanded or compressed depends on how inherently elastic it is. This elasticity is implemented as a parameter that controls the steepness of

[1]There is a strand of research that assumes that changes in speaking rate, specifically decreases in speaking rate, are driven by a desire to enhance or exaggerate a given phonological contrast (e.g. Beckman et al. 2011). Although slowed speaking rate often occurs under conditions in which speakers are deliberately hyper-articulating their speech, I assume that decreases in speaking rate can also occur independently; that is, that speakers can control their rate of speech, e.g. when asked to match the beat of a metronome, without consciously trying to produce more intelligible speech.

a logistic curve. For example, the effect of force E acting on the overlap variable (x^O) is given in Equation (6.2):

(6.2) $$SpeakingRate : x_i^{O''} = \frac{A}{(1 + e^{kE})}$$

A is a normalization factor, and is set to $2x_i^{Z'}$ for all variables (Z). This has the effect of making the adjusted length depend on the current length, with $E = 0$ resulting in no change. Note that for decreases in speaking rate, overlap should decrease – pulling the two gestures apart, and thus lengthening the word –, while for increases in speaking rate, overlap should increase. Therefore, the dependence of overlap on expansion degree is expressed as a positive exponential, while the dependence of the other two duration parameters is expressed as a negative exponential. For these simulations all three articulatory variables were set to the same elasticity ($k = 1$).

6.4 No-Phoneme Phoneme-Split Model

In order to understand the behavior of the phoneme-split models, we first create a version with only the speaking rate mechanism included. Figure 6.2 shows the outcome that the speaking rate distribution (E distribution) selects for, given a particular starting distribution of tokens. The three articulatory parameters are plotted separately, in different colors. This model also assumes error-free mapping of acoustics to articulation, outside of a small error term in production. Entrenchment and memory decay apply as in previous models.

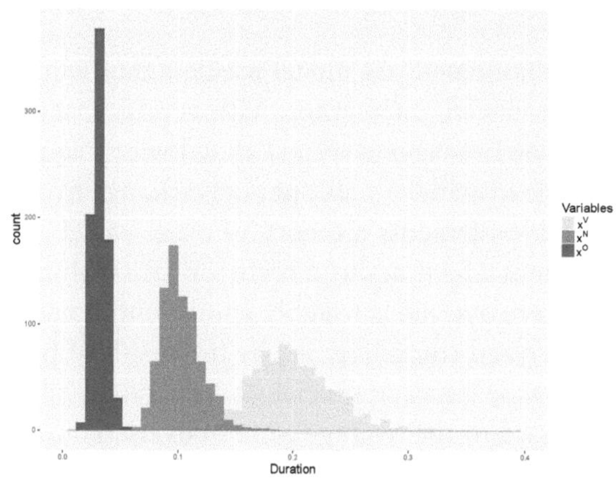

Figure 6.2: Phoneme-Split Model: Speaking rate only

With appropriately chosen constants, the speaking rate force is capable of disrupting the influence of the frequency-based attractor. This allows the equilibrium state of the model to vary as a function of word frequency (β). For $T = x_i^N$, the fluency effect acts consistently to increase gestural overlap ($T = x_i^N$). If it is too weak (β too small), then the speaking rate equilibrium shown in Figure 6.2 prevails. If it is strong enough, then it is able to shift the overlap distribution to larger values (rightward). This is possible because the speaking rate transform depends on the current value of the overlap parameter for any given token (expressed in the variable A of Eq. 6.2). Figure 6.3 shows the output of the model with both speaking rate and frequency bias, run for three different values of β. Note that the number of model iterations is essentially arbitrary. Because the number is large (10,000), there is a reasonable expectation that a stable state has been reached, but no tests of convergence were performed. In this section I am more concerned with the qualitative behavior of the model, and comparisons in which all but one aspect of the simulations are kept constant.

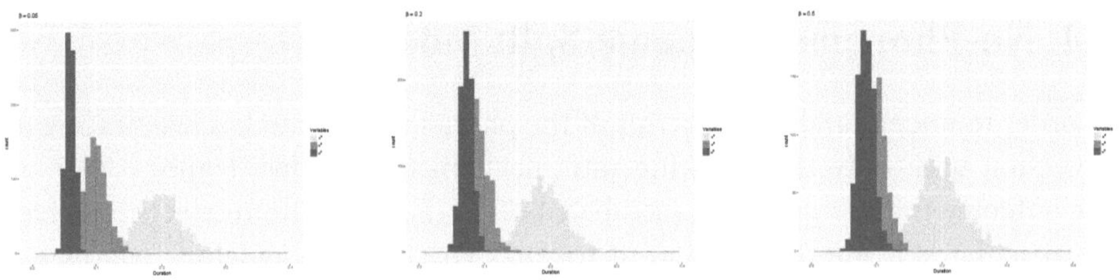

(a) Low-frequency word ($\beta = 0.05$)

(b) Mid-frequency word ($\beta = 0.2$)

(c) High-frequency word ($\beta = 0.5$)

Figure 6.3: No-Phoneme Phoneme-Split Model (Frequency Attractor). Each model run for 10,000 cycles with identical starting conditions.

The No-Phoneme Phoneme-Split model predicts that words with higher frequencies should be produced, on average, with vowels that are more nasalized (larger degree of overlap between gestures), than lower frequency words. It also shows that it is possible to achieve stable phonetic change from a change in word frequency. The model implements a theory of nasal vowel genesis as an emergent property of gradient effects acting directly on articulatory parameters. Only in the special case where overlap is roughly equivalent to nasal duration, would the data likely be analyzed (by a linguist) as the result of phoneme split. This state in the model, however, has no special status. And distributions that appear intermediate with regard to the average ratio of overlap duration to velum gesture duration can be stable. Conceptualizing phoneme split in this way allows us to avoid the actuation paradox that requires the loss of the conditioning environment, but the retention of the conditioned allophone (see Section 1.2). In fact, as there are no phoneme-level representations in this model, there are no allophones, and no conditioning environments, in the classical sense. Therefore, this model is also a demonstration that phoneme-level representations are not necessary (nor is any misperception/misarticulation pressure of the kind discussed in the previous chapter), to achieve a working model with the generally correct behavior.

The source of the nasalization effect in this model is the coordination between the tongue body and velum gestures. This parameter, however, is part of the underlying specification of each word token. The No-Phoneme model is thus a STATE model. Arguably, a STATE model represents a change that has already taken place, in which a process of nasalization has been reinterpreted as a static property of a unitary representation. In the next sections I will turn to a PROCESS model of vowel nasalization, returning to the misperception/misarticulation actuation mechanism. This will also involve introducing a sub-lexical level of representation, and revisiting the implementation of word frequency.

6.5 Parsing and misparsing

In order to recover the meaning of a given speech signal, it is necessary, at minimum, to identify the individual lexical items present. This, in turn, requires determining where one word ends and the next begins. The highly context-sensitive nature of acoustic cues, as well as the lack of consistent silence, or other markers, of the boundaries between words or sounds, make this a computationally difficult task. And this is not just an acquisition problem. Signal parsing, or segmentation, is something that must be carried out every time speech is perceived.

That segmentation of some kind must also take place at the sub-lexical level is evidenced by a large literature on what are known as "trading relations", in which the value along a given phonetic dimension that separates two members of a phonemic contrast is shown to vary depending on the values of the other phonetic cues present. And those other cues that influence the boundary location are not just those that occur within the segment itself. For example, a given phone ([t]) may be ambiguous as to whether it belongs with a preceding or following word (e.g. *great ship* [ɡɹe͡ɪt#ʃɪp] versus *gray chip* [ɡɹe͡ɪ#t͡ʃɪp]), and the actual word sequence that is heard will depend on the durations of the surrounding segments; longer durations of [e͡ɪ] increase the likelihood of *gray* over *great*, while shorter durations of [ʃ] increase the likelihood of *chip* over *ship*. An acoustic cue (such as silence itself) may also be ambiguous as to whether it originates from a phoneme (/t/) or a break between words (*great ship* versus *gray ship* [gɹe͡ɪ#ʃɪp]; longer durations of silence increase the likelihood of *great* over *gray* (Repp et al. 1978). An acoustic feature may also be ambiguous as to whether it belongs to a preceding segment, a following segment, or both ([ɹa͡ɪpbɛɹiz] as either *right berries* or *ripe berries*, Gow 2003).

In all of the preceding examples the ambiguity exists because of the existence of multiple real-word alternatives. Without those alternatives, or competitors, phonetically ambiguous input quickly becomes perceptually unambiguous (e.g. Warren 1970; Ganong 1980). The strong susceptibility of low-level perception to high-level expectations also speaks to the amount of noise, or essentially unpredictable variability, in the acoustic realization of a given abstract category. Speech perception involves the complex integration of multiple cues, each of which, in isolation, may be relatively uninformative, in order to arrive at a single parse, a single percept, of what is heard. This percept is presumably the best alternative among those available to the listener (see Davis & Johnsrude 2007 for a review of the literature). Although speech perception appears extremely robust due to the fact that the meaning intended by the speaker is usually recoverable by the listener, that robustness is a property of the entire set of cues available, not of acoustic features alone, and certainly not of individual acoustic features. Rather than conceptualizing sound change as the relatively rare event in which the listener mishears, or the speaker misspeaks, it may be the case that what we typically think of as the "changed" variants are already present within the distribution of stored tokens, as one of multiple possible parses of each inherently ambiguous input signal.

6.6 Multiple parses

The classical way in which sound change is conceptualized is based on the assumption that there exists a unique, correct, sub-lexical representation for each word. It is meaningless to speak of phoneme-level "errors" unless this is the case. Consider the following hypothetical example (where $x > y$ indicates an historical change from x to y):

(6.3) *anpa* > *ampa*

(6.3) is a common type of change known as nasal place assimilation. In this example, the coronal feature of the nasal /*n*/ is assimilated to (or replaced by) the labial feature of the following /*p*/. Speakers of a language that undergoes this change presumably had an earlier allophonic rule specifying that /*n*/'s preceding stops take on the place features of that stop. Therefore, the change could only have occurred if they uncharacteristically failed to account for this rule, or they made the "wrong" choice for a production that was especially strongly assimilated. In either case, listeners are assumed to parse their acoustic input into a sequence of discrete phones, deciding for each segment whether to normalize or accept at face value. Thus, for a change from */anpa/* to */ampa/* to have actually occurred in the way it is denoted here, it must be the case that listeners used to routinely segment continuous acoustic tokens of this word into the sequence of units */a/*, */n/*, */p/*, */a/*, until they switched to segmenting those tokens into the sequence */a/*, */m/*, */p/*, */a/*.

Of course, we know that a discrete series of abstract symbols (either *[anpa]* or *[ampa]*) is not present in the acoustic signal in any objective sense. The abstract notation also implies that this change occurs once, simultaneously, for all words, and for all word tokens. However, adopting the hypothesis that multiple experienced instances of speech are stored implies that change would have to occur over individual tokens. In fact, the multiple-parse hypothesis is a logical consequence of the basic tenet of the exemplar framework. The conflation of perception and production that we saw in the exemplar models of Chapters 2 and 4 is borrowed directly from the standard generative notation. Once a transformation from perceptual tokens to production tokens is required, it becomes clear that 1) parsing is necessary in the first place, and 2) it must occur for each experienced token. Recognizing that acoustic tokens are inherently ambiguous with respect to their decomposition into discrete units suggests, in turn, that variable parses might be the norm rather than the exception.[2]

In the nasal assimilation example, there are two obvious alternative parses, differing in whether they contain the phoneme /*n*/ or /*m*/, thus the word-level category *anpa* is hypothesized to be composed of at least some tokens specified with production targets for /*n*/, and some for /*m*/. However, additional possible parses exist if we do not assume the available phoneme inventory *a priori*. In fact, if we allow all universally possible segments into the analysis space, then we avoid the actuation paradox of the classical diachronic approach. As the next section will show, this re-framing of the change question allows synchronic variation to be linked to diachronic change in a way that is not dependent on either stopping or starting the model at a critical point in time.

[2]This is closely related to the proposal that stored lexical items can have more than one representation (see e.g. Hooper 1976; Janda 2008; Bybee 2001). Split representations are also assumed to be the outcome of discontinuous articulatory change in the model of Garrett & Johnson (2013).

6.7 Representations II

The Multiple-Parse model adds a PROCESS component to the No-Phoneme model. The process is implemented at the level of the articulatory gesture, but conceptually requires the existence of abstract categories intermediate between the word and the gesture. As before, the change occurs in the distribution of variants that already exist, rather than in the genesis of entirely novel forms. This aspect bears some similarity to the proposal in Baker et al. (2011), based on misanalysis of the signal, but the current model is not abrupt, nor does it require "extreme" variants to be adopted.

The conversion from perception to production is the locus of sub-lexical parsing, mapping every continuous acoustic token into a series of categorical units. In principle, these units can consist of any contiguous set as long as it is phonetically plausible, and exhaustively parses the input signal. However, in the case of vowel nasalization, I will be concerned with two particular possibilities: the one-sublexical-unit analysis, and the two-sublexical-unit analysis. These are of special interest, of course, because they bear considerable similarity to the classical analyses of the phenomenon before change (two units), and after change (one unit). However, it is important to be very careful in how these units are described, because the traditional notational system essentially forces an analysis more general than the word level. In order not to assume generalization, and remain representationally consistent, the following notation will be adopted for the two sub-lexical parses of the word in question (*am*): $/\tilde{V}_{am}/$ (Analysis 1), and $/V_{am}/ + /N_{am}/$ (Analysis 2). The desired implication is that only after generalization across multiple words could something similar to the abstract categories $/\widetilde{V}/$ and $/V/ + /N/$ arise.

For the articulatory parameters already defined, a single-unit parse means that all three values will be stored on the production side. $/\tilde{V}_{am}/$ is a 3-dimensional cloud, and entrenchment applies over each dimension. Note that this is what was assumed for all tokens in the No-Phoneme Model, which therefore implicitly assumed a single-unit analysis. The two-unit parse, however, is explicitly a PROCESS analysis, entailing that one token is drawn from a one-dimensional $/V_{am}/$ cloud, one from a one-dimensional $/N_{am}/$ cloud, with concatenation occurring at the time of production. In other words, the overlap between the two gestures is not stored, but determined online.

6.8 Multiple-Parse Phoneme-Split Model

Either analysis is possible for any given token, but, critically, depends on the acoustic properties of that token. In this set of simulations it will be assumed that word-level categorization is correct, and that the three duration quantities (x_i^V, x_i^N, x_i^O) are accurately recovered in perception, although this is not critical.[3] Analysis 1, the single-segment analysis, is more likely to be selected, the more highly overlapped the gestures that produced that token, while Analysis 2, the 2-segments-in-sequence analysis, is more likely for less overlapped gestures. The specific dependence is on the quantity $Q_i = x_i^O / x_i^N$. Larger values of x_i^O lead to larger values of Q_i, as do smaller values of x_i^N. Selecting for large Q thus selects both for larger overlap and shorter word durations. That duration should correlate with number of constituents is a reasonable hypothesis. It can also be hypothesized that articulatory gestures will tend to be more tightly coordinated within, than across, segments, if shared constituency promotes greater merger.[4] The probability of Analysis 1, $P(a = 1)$, depends on Q in the following way (6.4).

$$P(a = 1) = Ae^{-b(1-Q)} - C \quad (6.4)$$

Probability increases with increasing Q because of the negative exponential in (6.4). The largest possible value for Q is 1, therefore $1 - Q$ is always positive. When $Q = 1$, $P(a = 1)$ reaches its maximum at $A - C$. How quickly the probability decreases as a function of decreasing Q is controlled by the variable b. The larger b, the larger the negative exponential, and the more quickly $P(a = 1)$ decreases, selecting for larger mean Q values (and fewer tokens). See Appendix E for additional details.

If Analysis 1 is chosen in perception, based on the value of $P(a = 1)$, then all three values of the token are stored. If Analysis 2 is chosen, then the duration of the tongue body gesture (x_i^V), and the duration of the velum gesture (x_i^N), are each stored in separate categories, and the overlap value is discarded. Figure 6.4 provides a schematic depiction of these relationships. Note that the dimensions are not accurately represented here; two dimensions are used for all categories to make the membership relationships easier to see. Individual tokens are drawn as schematic gestural scores: extent represents time, and fill type represents active

[3]If the error term is symmetrical, then it will have no qualitative effect on the model dynamics.

[4]I am not aware of evidence for this specific relationship, but there is evidence for different types of gestural coordination across different domains: between the onset and nucleus of a syllable, versus the nucleus and coda (Browman & Goldstein 1988; Byrd 1996); and within, versus across, morpheme boundaries (Cho 2001).

articulator. Where the two bars appear together, horizontal alignment indicates the stored gestural overlap parameter. The thin lines drawn between tokens of different sub-categories indicate that they are stored together, and will be produced together. However, overlap must be determined separately because it is not stored as part of the experienced token. Entrenchment happens only within individual sub-lexical categories.[5]

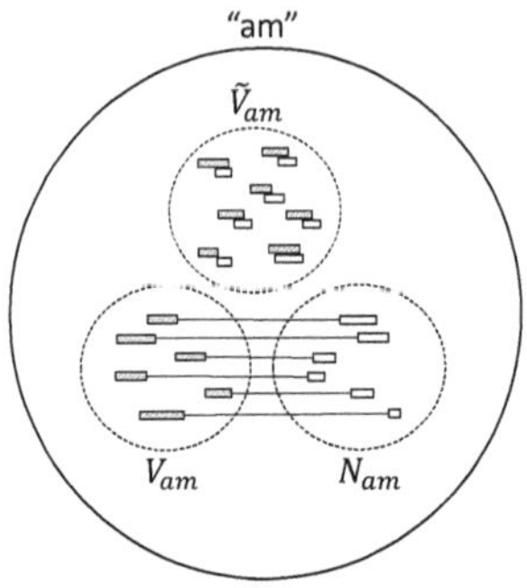

Figure 6.4: Schematic depiction of the relationships between the word-level category (*am*) and the sub-lexical level categories of its constituents. Production-side representations.

Tokens are chosen randomly for production from among all stored values. Once selected, the token is subject to the same speaking rate transformation used in the No-Phoneme model. The overlap degree for an Analysis-2 token defaults to a fixed percentage of the current average value of x^N (with some variance). There is no phonetic bias in this model. The selection bias that drives the feedback loop resides in the choice of underlying analysis – the parsing of the input signal. Equation 6.4 selects for large values of x^O, and for small values of x^N, both of which will increase the size of Q, and thus increase the probability of Analysis 1. There is no cumulativity such that these values grow more extreme, but there is a constant pressure to sort tokens with the largest overlap proportion into this sub-lexical category. Thus, if an independent mechanism resulted in an increase in Q for some tokens, those tokens would raise the average Q value of the $/\tilde{V}_{am}/$ sub-category.

[5]If entrenchment at the word level is added it will have the effect of pushing values back towards the means of the Analysis 2 categories, since the model is initialized with those values, and the Analysis 2 parse is always more likely.

A mechanism that shortens word duration will have this effect: shortening x^N (and x^V), and lengthening x^O. If higher frequency is taken to result in faster productions, then an increase in frequency will lead both to more $/\tilde{V}_{am}/$ categorizations, and to a higher Q value for the category on average. For the simulations reported below, frequency was implemented as a negative perturbation to the mean value of the expansion force distribution. As a result, higher frequency (higher resting activation) results in shorter words, and thus shorter tongue body and velum gestures (and longer overlap) under all speaking rates. This implementation will be discussed in more detail in the following section.

Figure 6.5 shows the model results as a function of frequency. Each point is the result of running the model for 10,000 iterations. Mean values for the three duration parameters, as well as the proportion overlap (Q) are given for each of the categories - Panel 1: word-level; Panel 2: Analysis 1 tokens; Panel 3: Analysis 2 tokens. Note that the overlap proportion in Panel 3 shows the constraint that overlap proportion stay fixed with respect to $\overline{x^N}$. Whereas, in Panel 2, as resting activation (frequency) increases, the proportion overlap increases. Because the number of tokens parsed into the $/\tilde{V}_{am}/$ category also increases with increasing resting activation (from approximately 31% to 50%), the overlap proportion increases for the word-level category as a whole (Panel 1).

6.9 Frequency II

In the No-Phoneme Phoneme-Split model, frequency was implemented as a fixed attractor on overlap duration (Section 6.2). The assumption was that there existed an optimal (most fluent) production of a given word with precisely the degree of gestural overlap given by the attractor target. At the same time, in order to generate productions that more closely resembled nasal vowels, it was necessary to set the target quite high – in the reported simulations it was set to the entire duration of the accompanying velum gesture. However, it is not clear why the optimal production of the 2-gesture word should exhibit such a large degree of overlap. And, in general, there is no clear reason for greater practice, or increased fluency, to always result in shortened, or reduced, articulations, especially to the point where distinctiveness may be lost at the word and/or phoneme level. Yet this seems to be the case with frequency effects. It has been shown, for example, that individual segments within high-frequency words are shorter, and that they are more likely to exhibit "deletions" (dropping, or masking of a consonant, or unstressed vowel, e.g. Bell et al. 2003; Raymond et al. 2006; Bybee 2003). The realizations of segments in higher-frequency words tend also to be less extreme,

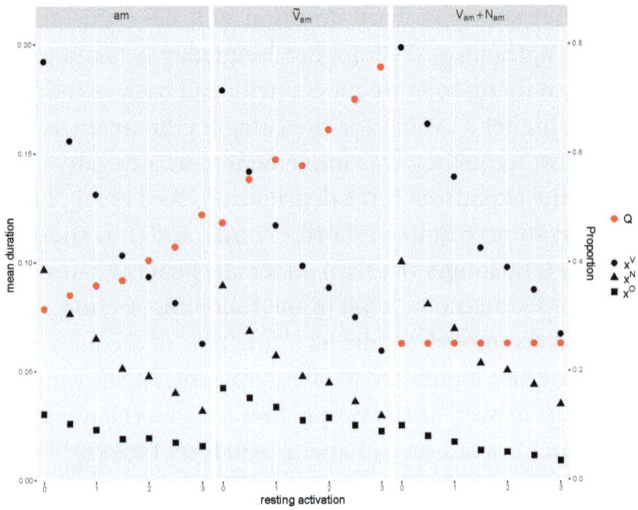

Figure 6.5: Multiple-Parse Model: Results as a function of resting activation (word frequency). Each point corresponds to the mean after 10,000 model iterations. Mean articulatory durations are plotted in black. Proportion overlap ($Q = \overline{x^O}/\overline{x^N}$) is plotted in red. Panel 1: all word tokens; Panel 2: Analysis-1 tokens only; Panel 3: Analysis-2 tokens only.

or more "centralized", perhaps failing to reach the usual articulatory target (e.g. Munson & Solomon 2004; Scarborough 2004; Gahl 2008).

The listener-based account of frequency effects explains these phenomena as a consequence of contextual predictability. It is actually the less predictable, less easy to access, more confusable, forms that are produced with particular care (hyper-articulated) by the speaker in order to aid intelligibility (e.g. Aylett & Turk 2004). In the absence of that pressure, articulations are reduced to the degree possible, facilitating the task of the speaker. Factors that have been shown to affect predictability, as well as word form, include sentence, or discourse, context, bigram frequency, and unigram frequency, among others. Nevertheless, there are a number of results that are not compatible with a strictly listener-based theory, studies that have shown that speakers do not always alter their productions in such a way as to facilitate listener comprehension (see Turnbull 2015 for a review of the literature).

As mentioned briefly in Section 3.1, the speaker-based approach attributes frequency effects to automatic production-side mechanisms. This is usually couched in terms of activation levels, within some kind of lexical network model where different representations "compete" in both perception and production (e.g. McClelland & Rumelhart 1981; Dell 1986). In terms of word retrieval, the successful candidate is the one that achieves a given threshold of activation first. Every time a word is accessed, or produced, it is activated to this level. Repeated activations, within some time period, are taken to result in some level of residual activation that persists even when the word is not selected. This "resting" activation level is naturally higher in higher frequency words, giving them a head start against lower-frequency competitors.

The resting-activation account is in line with results establishing that higher-frequency words are produced earlier than lower-frequency ones in a variety of tasks, such as picture naming, and word or sentence reading – even with delays. Higher-frequency words also lead to faster response times in lexical decision and other speeded response tasks, as well as to greater accuracy in word recognition (e.g. Howes & Solomon 1951; Balota & Chumbley 1985; Luce 1986; Marslen-Wilson 1990). However, it is not at all obvious that higher resting activation alone can account for articulatory or temporal reduction (hypo-articulation).

In fact, it has been argued *both* that a higher activation level should lead to hyper-articulation (e.g. Baese-Berk & Goldrick 2009), and that it should lead to hypo-articulation (e.g. Gahl et al. 2012).[6] In works that adopt the latter position, the connection seems to be assumed. For example, Gahl et al. (2012: 79) write that "Production-based accounts ... would lead one to expect that words that are retrieved quickly tend to be phonetically reduced – *provided that fast retrieval speed translates into fast production speed*" (emphasis mine).

The fact that there does not appear to be a well-worked out mechanism for this result raises the possibility that we have yet to find the right model for frequency. Empirically, however, the correlation between shorter/faster productions and higher word frequency seems quite robust. In the Multiple-Parse Model, a frequency-based increase in production speed is taken to be an additive effect, acting to effectively shift the speaking rate distribution. If I continue to assume that speaking rate acts independently of other model forces, then words will continue to be pulled in both directions, expanding or compressing in turn. Subject to the same large positive force, both low and high frequency words will be produced more slowly, and will thus be longer than if no force had applied. However, the high-frequency word will be somewhat shorter than its low frequency counterpart, due to the difference in its resting state. The same will be found under compression (unless floor is reached).

[6]Note that different results were obtained in these studies, one based on laboratory data, and one on conversational corpus data.

The dependence on frequency (resting activation) in Figure 6.5 shows the effect of progressively shifting the speaking rate distribution; shorter average word durations result in shorter x^N, and longer x^O, and thus lead to a greater proportion of Analysis 1 tokens.[7] This shift is not unbounded, because speaking rate is a bi-directional force; high-frequency words can also be lengthened, just not lengthened quite as much as their lower-frequency counterparts. Note that the frequency effect in this model acts on all tokens, both stored and generated. In the latter case, we must assume that some type of motor plan involving the concatenation of $/V_{am}/$ and $/N_{am}/$ is associated with a resting activation value that affects the duration of the resulting word.

6.10 Actuation

As in the No-Phoneme Phoneme Split model, there is no single moment at which a sound change occurs in the Multiple-Parse Phoneme-Split Model. Every instance of perception involves a decision about parsing which is based on existing synchronic variation. And every available parse is a possibility at any time, for any token; it is the probabilities of those parses which change over time. Although the nasal vowel parse is assumed in the sense that it is one possible analysis for a given token, this model, in fact, avoids many limiting assumptions about the nature of sound change inherent to the classical view. For example, the */V+N/* analysis is not privileged, beyond having a higher probability of selection, given the starting distribution. Additional analyses can be added to the set of parsing hypotheses, if motivated by general-purpose properties of speech perception. It is consistently the word level at which all forces act in this model, and at the level of articulatory gesture that changes are realized. In particular, this model does not rely on the allophonic level at which the synchronic rule, and the diachronic change, are assumed to occur. As a result, the normalization/lack of normalization question becomes a basic element of speech processing: the analysis that must occur when perceptual values are transformed into production values.

If classification occurs at the word level, and words have articulatory representations something like gestural scores, then it is not necessary to first identify a series of abstract phonemes in order to identify individual words. Thus, the problem of "compensating" for (the feature of) nasalization at the level of the

[7] Because the duration of overlap cannot exceed the length of the shortest gesture, the longest *absolute* overlap durations can only occur with the longest word tokens, thus there is also some selection pressure towards longer x^N inherent in the x^O measure. Reducing the length of x^N will therefore eliminate some of the largest x^O tokens.

phoneme disappears. The ambiguity remains regarding the proper articulatory realization of a given acoustic input, but there is no longer a unique, correct sublexical analysis. The possible analyses available to the listener, based on their phonetic experience, should always include, at minimum, both the "normalized" option, as well as the "unnormalized" one.

In the specific simulations reported in the previous section, the average percentage of the velum lowering gesture that occurred simultaneously with the tongue body gesture varied from 30%, for the lowest-frequency word, to about 50% for the highest-frequency word. It was also the case that absolute gesture durations were considerably shorter at higher frequencies. These results describe a diachronic change under the scenario in which a single word comes to be used more, or less, frequently over time. Under the scenario in which frequencies are fixed, but there exists a set of words with a range of different frequencies, these results describe a synchronic distribution. The model thus generates at least two testable predictions: 1) that a difference in the degree of vowel nasalization should be observed across words of different frequencies (provided the relevant phonological context is sufficiently similar among those words), and 2) that the highest-frequency words should approximate the degree of vowel nasalization observed in languages that are described as having phonemically nasal vowels. In other words, no exaggeration, or enhancement, of the effect is required in this model. Lexicon-wide change is assumed to start with change at the individual word level.

It is widely acknowledged that change (of certain kinds, at least) happens on a word by word basis (e.g. Phillips 1984; Bybee 2002; Pierrehumbert 2002), and that some words can be "further along" in the change than others. With regards to nasalized vowels in particular, Malécot (1960) offers evidence that the distinction between English words like *cap* and *camp* is primarily that between a nasal and oral vowel ([kæp] vs. [kæ̃p]), rather than the presence versus absence of a nasal consonant ([kæp] vs. [kæ̃mp]). The English segmental inventory is not usually analyzed as containing an abstract nasal vowel (although see Solé 1992 for an argument that nasal vowels are phonologically specified). Nevertheless, individual tokens, or individual words, or even classes of words, may have phonetic realizations that are indistinguishable from those generated from an underlying nasal vowel.

7 Discussion & conclusions

7.1 Of words, phonemes and allophones

The aim of Chapter 6 was to develop an explanatory model of a specific type of sound change: phoneme split, or phoneme genesis. Yet, in the course of developing that model, the change being modeled itself underwent a certain kind of transformation. When phoneme split was first introduced in Section 1.2 it was described as allophone becoming phoneme. The implication, particularly in the case of vowel nasalization, was that a completely new phoneme category had to be created, something that had not been previously modeled. The classical representations for the synchronic and diachronic rules are given below.

(7.1) $/V/ \rightarrow [\tilde{V}]/\_N$

(7.2) (a) $/VN/ > /\tilde{V}/$

(b) $[\tilde{V}] > /\tilde{V}/$

In scenario (7.2 a), the loss of the nasal context *(N)* is the precipitating event, critical to the emergence of the phoneme. In scenario (7.2 b) the loss of the nasal context is irrelevant; the phoneme arises through some other mechanism.

Immediately, the actuation problem arises – the problem of determining why phoneme split sometimes happens and sometimes does not (Weinreich et al. 1968). If the conditioning context can be lost without phoneme genesis, then it cannot be the loss alone that creates the phoneme (7.2 a). But if the loss of context is irrelevant and coincidental, then contextually predictable phonemes are possible and we have no way to determine, or predict, the status of such sounds (7.2 b).

The solution to this impasse suggested by the Multiple-Parse Model is that phonemes are nothing other than hypotheses made by individual listener/speakers about how to break up word-level units, hypotheses that may change from moment to moment and from token to token. Once such a hypothesis is made it acquires its own representational reality – at least for that listener/speaker. Because allophonic relationships only exist as corollaries of a given phonemic analysis, they are automatically generated under one hypothesis, and automatically missing under the other.

However, even under the "allophonic" analysis, allophones never actually surface in this model. The process that generates what linguists would label as an allophone does not occur at the same representational level as the phoneme; it occurs in the region shared between two adjacent phonemes.[1] It is predictable in the sense that nasality is predictable when the velum is lowered. But it is meaningless to talk about bigram predictability – the predictability of vowel nasality from the subsequent nasal – because the listener does not hear a sequence of phones. Under one parsing of the input, nasality will be attributed to gestural overlap between adjacent phonemes, under another it will be attributed to gestural overlap within a single phoneme. In either case it will be entirely predictable.

The sound change in question, therefore, does not actually involve the generation of a new phoneme category. If I assume that all possible hypotheses are entertained for all ambiguous inputs, then all phonemes exist at all times, and it is only their probabilities that might change over time.[2] This reframing avoids the representational paradoxes discussed earlier. Actuation now pertains to factors that affect the probability distribution over the hypothesis space. Such factors are likely to be numerous, and undoubtedly include aspects of language processing not explored here. In the same vein, the vowel nasalization model is not to be taken as applicable to all types of sound change, nor even as a model of all aspects of vowel nasalization change. In the next two sections some other factors are briefly discussed, along with possible extensions of the current work.

7.2 Additional implications & future work

The Multiple-Parse Model is a model of the internal dynamics of a single word category in isolation. In this model the assumption is that sub-lexical categories are derived from words, rather than the other way around (see, e.g. Beckman & Edwards 2000). Once such categories arise, however, they are expected to exert influence in the other direction (English orthography is likely to produce a similar effect). Even without the influence of explicit phoneme categories, we expect word-level representations to be linked in some way that reflects their similar-

[1]Incidentally, this reveals another hidden assumption of the generative notation: the fact that coarticulation appears to only affect one of the segments involved. Nasalization occurs on the vowel, but vocalization should also occur on the nasal. This bias is most likely based in perception, but articulation-wise, the allophonic relationship may be relatively symmetric.

[2]This does not preclude the merger of phonetic values in the pronunciation of two sounds that were previously distinct (e.g. the so-called PIN/PEN merger in certain dialects of American English).

ity to each other. Therefore, the evolution of a given word cannot truly occur in isolation.

Sound change is typically taken to refer to change at the phoneme level. In the Multiple-Parse Model change is taken to occur at a less abstract level: sublexical, but specific to an individual word. I assume that a generalization stage is necessary, likely requiring multiple, semi-independent changes at the word level.[3] The dynamics of such a model are not trivial, and require, among other constraints, that the phoneme-to-word feedback bias be strong enough to allow generalization to occur across all words containing that phoneme, but not so strong as to prevent changes at the level of the individual word.

One interesting consequence of adopting the position that word categories precede phoneme categories, is that phonetic regularities must begin as STATES (stored articulatory variables), rather than PROCESSES (the result of combining two or more linguistic units), in the infant learner. Processes are potentially inferred gradually, over sufficient amounts of variable data (e.g. Bates & Goodman 1997), but individual STATE representations might persist, as PROCESS ones do in the simulations of the previous section.

The opposite course of development might be expected to occur in the domain of morphology, where explicit concatenation requires a PROCESS model, but STATE analyses become available over time. In fact, the "competition" between the Analysis-1 parse and the Analysis-2 parse bears a high degree of similarity to dual-route theories of morphology (e.g. Caramazza et al. 1988; Frauenfelder & Schreuder 1992). Classically, transparent morphological alternations are assumed to be rule-based, analogously to allophonic alternations. However, it is evident from the historical record that morphological affixations that were once productive can fall out of use, resulting in a few artifactual forms that are unlikely to be decomposed into their constituents by modern speakers. Additionally, some highly frequent forms, although transparently decomposable, may behave as though they have unique lexical entries (e.g. Baayen et al. 1997.[4]) This parallelism does not seem to be coincidental, and is especially relevant to allophonic alternations that occur precisely at morpheme boundaries.

Morphophonological alternations are, in fact, often taken to comprise the best evidence of an active phonological rule. This is because the morphological process involved is assumed to be productive. That is, it is assumed to be a PROCESS. Yet, the change that led to the phonological alternation may only have come

[3]Not to mention the spread of change to all members of a speech community, which I assume is another necessary stage of change, but well beyond the scope of the present work.

[4]See Levelt et al. 1999 for a review of frequency-based storage, and Burani & Caramazza 1987; Baayen 1993 for further discussion of factors affecting morphological storage.

about due to representations becoming more STATE-like, as is implied by the behavior of the Multiple-Parse Model. If this is on the right track, then truly phonological, truly productive alternations may only arise when STATE and PROCESS representations are balanced in such a way as to preserve this tension. Determining the necessary conditions for this to happen presents an interesting area for future research.

7.3 Types of sound change

In the modeling of sound change, the term "phonetic bias" seems to have been used as a cover term to refer to phonetically-based sound change of more or less any kind. Thus it has been (or can be) applied to word reduction, vowel lengthening, vowel nasalization, and nasal place assimilation (or loss), among others. However, there is no *a priori* reason to expect all phonetically-based sound change to operate in the same way. And part of an ultimate theory of sound change will include a taxonomy both of the source of a given change, as well as its actuation mechanism.

The Multiple-Parse Model of vowel nasalization presented in Chapter 6 is based on the hypothesis that coarticulatory nasalization is *not* best analyzed as a phonetic bias; that is, as a constant pressure acting in a fixed direction. Instead, the source of nasalization is taken to be an inherent property of motor planning involving the temporal overlap between adjacent articulatory gestures. Synchronically, overlap degree is assumed to vary as a function of speaking rate, among potentially many factors, all of them contributing to a stable distribution with a certain degree of variance. In the implemented model, a change in the resting activation of a word-level category acts to shift both the absolute durations of the articulatory parameters, as well as the proportion of overlap. Words become shorter, with a higher degree of overlap, as resting activation increases. This follows from the assumption that activation level directly affects not only the speed with which words are accessed and initiated, but also the speed at which articulation unfolds. The utility of this model is only as good as this assumption, and will need to be revised if our understanding of the frequency effect changes.[5] However, actuation is achievable by any mechanism that can shift the overlap distribution as a whole.

[5]The correlation between speaking rate and degree of coarticulation, as well as the correlation between word-frequency and degree of coarticulation, appear to be quite robust. It is less clear, however, what the exact mechanism is that mediates between activation level and degree of coarticulation. Without this link, we run the risk of modeling an epiphenomenon, rather than the phenomenon itself.

The Multiple-Parse Model, of course, is meant to be not just a model of vowel nasalization, but of all linguistic phenomena that are functionally equivalent to vowel nasalization. Establishing this class is not trivial, and I will only hypothesize here that phenomena involving articulatory overlap, articulatory blending, and articulatory masking will generally be possible to model in this way. True phonetic biases can also be incorporated into the general model. Consonants occurring before other consonants (rather than vowels) can be considered to be in a perceptually disadvantaged position. This is especially true for stops, since most of the cues to their identity actually occur in the transitions to a following vowel (e.g. Liberman et al. 1954), but likely holds to some extent for most consonants. Articulatorily, the velum gesture attributed to the nasal in a word like *camp* will be overlapped to some extent not only with the preceding vowel, but also with the following consonant. The overlap with the preceding vowel is highly audible, while the overlap with the following stop is much less so, due to the complete closure in the oral cavity. The stop context, relative to a vowel context (such as in the word *camo*), can be thought of as biasing for nasal deletion (or a nasal vowel). This can be implemented as a factor that raises the probability of the single-segment parse.[6]

Velar palatalization was briefly discussed in Section 5.3 as an example of gesture blending. Faster productions will result in more overlap between consonant and vowel, which should merge the two gestures more completely, as well as render the combined production shorter. Both phonetic properties should lead to an increase in the probability of the single-segment analysis. The many different ways in which palatalization can be realized in different languages (e.g. k>t͡ʃ, k>k^j, kj>k^j, etc.) suggests a number of possible influencing factors, as well as an inherently larger space of possible parses. One such parse results in a two-segment analysis, with an intermediate tongue position for the consonantal gesture (see Figure 5.2b); another results in a single-segment analysis with a complex two-target gesture (see Figure 5.3). Perceptual asymmetries have been found with respect to the rate of misidentification of [ki] sequences in noise and fast speech (as [ti] and [t͡ʃi], most commonly) suggesting that phonetic bias plays a role in this change (Guion 1998; Chang et al. 2001).

[6]In fact, the word-final context modeled in Chapter 6 does not constitute a homogeneous phonetic environment. Unless the target word is in absolute phrase-final position it will be followed by another word, beginning with either a consonant or a vowel. Because the two different possibilities consist of different perceptual environments, segment loss might only occur in the former, resulting in a type of liaison (e.g. Tranel 1981). There is also some evidence to suggest that changes restricted to specific words can be attributed to their historically higher occurrence rates in the perceptually disadvantaged environment (e.g. Brown & Raymond 2012).

In contrast, the phenomenon of vowel lengthening (Section 3.2) does not appear to be the direct result of overlap, blending, or masking. There is, however, no consensus in the literature regarding the phonetic source of this effect. In fact, there is not even agreement about whether the process is one of lengthening before voiced obstruents, or shortening before voiceless ones (Gimson 1970; Wells 1982). Of the hypotheses proposed, most have an articulatory basis (e.g. Belasco 1958; Delattre 1962; Chen 1970; Lisker 1974; Klatt 1976; Moreton 2004; Schwartz 2010), but auditory/perceptual accounts have been offered as well (e.g. Lisker 1957; Javkin 1977; Kluender et al. 1988). None of these have been firmly established empirically, and strong arguments have been made against many of them. Without some idea of what the mechanism for the actual increase (or decrease) in length is, it is not possible to produce an insightful model. Work in progress suggests, in fact, that the apparent lengthening effect may be epiphenomenal: the result of partial temporal compensation, resulting from an upper limit on the duration of voiced obstruents (Morley & Smith in prep.). If this is correct then it suggests another type of misparsing that can occur when multiple sources affect the same phonetic dimension in roughly the same way. In the case of vowel length, contributing sources include phrase-final lengthening, lengthening due to slowed speaking rate, and greater length due to an inherently longer vowel, creating ambiguity as to how the observed duration should be attributed.[7]

Other kinds of change, such as transphonologization, or chain shifting, suggest yet other potential sources, but it is beyond the scope of this book to speculate about their exact nature. However, given a hypothesis regarding the source of the phenomenon and the representational level at which it acts, it is possible to create an implemented model. Such a model may, or may not, bear much resemblance to those proposed in this work, yet the basic questions about the relationship between theory and model, and between model and implementation will remain the same.

7.4 Summary & conclusions

Computational models allow us to run experiments with language that are not possible in the real world, such as those at the timescale of diachronic change. They present a powerful and useful tool for making explicit tests of our current

[7]This theory requires that some type of normalization be carried out – even if it is just a comparison between neighboring segments. If pure duration is the dimension of contrast, then it is hard to see how segments could be classified as "long" or "short" unless speaking rate, at minimum, is taken into account.

theories. Computational models can be used to establish existence proofs, demonstrating that it is possible to solve a problem in a particular way. On the flip side, modeling requires extensive simplification of the complex factors at play in language use and comprehension and there is never any guarantee that the simplifications have not altered the problem to the point that the results no longer shed light on the phenomenon of interest. Implemented models are often tailored to specific problems, and may prove to be inconsistent with other known aspects of language. In order to get a model to run, there are various implementational choices that must be made, choices that may, in fact, contain hidden theoretical assumptions. Thus, the interpretation of modeling results, just like the interpretation of the more traditional type of experimental results, must include serious consideration of potential confounds.

The purpose of the present work has been to bring the theoretical issues to the fore via explicit links between different implementational approaches and the types of representational structures they embody. In this way a number of representational inconsistencies, or paradoxes, were uncovered. The more transparent of these were the cases in which tokens were assigned two different underlying representations, or where an explicitly separate (i.e. stored) category was also subject to a process, giving the phenomenon a hybrid STATE-PROCESS status. In fact, there may be a paradox lurking in applying a process (e.g. knowing that tokens should be lengthened in a particular context) but failing to account for the effects of that process (lengthening) when adding the produced token back to the perceptual exemplar cloud.

Two apparent successes of the basic iterative exemplar model – accounting for frequency-based lenition, and phonetic similarity effects – were called into question. Section 2.4.1 demonstrated that, depending on the specifics of how word frequency is represented, successive reduction of tokens does not necessarily produce the observed negative correlation between frequency and word length. Retention of fine-grained phonetic detail (without retention of production context) was shown to actually disrupt predictable phonetic allophony. Depending on other representational decisions, the result was either a single variant that occurred in all contexts, multiple variants that occurred unpredictably, or a continuously moving target (Section 2.4.2).

Developing exemplar models that make the right kinds of predictions requires some force for constraining the powerful iterativity mechanism of the perception-production feedback loop. This is often accomplished in practice by filtering out tokens that fall between two existing, contrastive categories. But in the absence of contrast, something else is required to keep the categories bounded. There seems to be a common misconception that exemplar models do not require underlying representations, or targets. But models may in fact implement what amounts functionally to a soft target, or attractor, even if it is not identified as such (Section 4.3). Such a target may, in fact, be necessary to produce bounded behavior.

Furthermore, the standard assumption of an identity mapping between perception and production obscures the complexity of the speech processing problem. In fact, differences between what speakers intend to produce, and what listeners perceive, are likely to play a large role in diachronic change that arises from synchronic variation, the very thing these models are trying to explain. Nor is it the case that iterative application of an articulation-based bias (such as anticipatory feature spread) can be assumed to lead to cumulativity on the acoustic side (Chapter 5). To produce the type of gradual increase that is desired, a change in the relative timing of articulators may be required. The explanation as to why such a change would occur is the answer to the actuation question itself.

A proposal was offered in Chapter 6 for one way to account for phoneme genesis arising from allophonic split. The model was designed in a way that prioritized representational consistency, capturing both change and stability, and implementing a plausible mechanism for change at both local and global scales. The "correct" sub-lexical representations were not assumed, and therefore, neither was the allophonic rule (or production bias). Instead, the equivalent of an articulatory representation was decided independently for each token. Feedback occurred in the dependence of the parsing probabilities on the values of the articulatory parameters. In the reported simulations there was only one choice to be made by the speaker/listener, whether to store or generate the degree of overlap between the two articulatory gestures. Stability was achieved by a general-purpose force (speaking rate), acting bi-directionally, to both lengthen and shorten tokens. Different stable states resulted from different resting activation levels, which affected the rapidity with which the words were produced. This result hinged on two properties of the model: the dependence of the speaking rate effect on word duration (longer tokens were lengthened more than shorter tokens for the same decrease in rate), and the implementation of resting activation as a shift in the mean of the speaking rate distribution. Numerous other implementational choices are possible, but only a small fraction of them lead to a theoretically coherent, cognitively plausible, empirically adequate outcome. Thus, the existence proof embodied in the Multiple-Parse Model has merit in and of itself. The results also raise the possibility that certain consistently intractable problems in the study of change and actuation may be artifacts of the overt and covert assumptions of the traditional notational system.

On the one hand, the work in this book represents relatively minor variations on existing proposals and models: the basic exemplar architecture in which subphonemic detail is retained; the role of word frequency in sound change; ambiguity in surface forms as the driver of variation; etc. Its primary innovation may be in bringing together and explicitly implementing those elements. Yet, the result is a radical re-conceptualization of basic phonological tenets. I have suggested that 1) phoneme split is neither phoneme creation, nor allophone loss, 2) neither allophonic rules nor phonemic inventories actually exist as traditionally described, and 3) phonological rules as we typically understand them may only arise under restricted conditions, requiring morphological antecedents and a more explicit stage of learner generalization. This conceptual shift was largely a consequence of forcing diachronic and synchronic representations to match, revealing that questions about how sound categories change are really questions about what sound categories are – how they are mentally represented –, and that neither question can be adequately answered without the other.

Appendix A: Model parameters: Chapters 1–4

For each of the basic exemplar models for which simulations were run, the following parameter values were used:

Table A.1: Simulation parameter values

	ε	σ_{error}	α	p	β	σ	N
Baseline Model (Chapter 2)	0.3	σ	0.1	–	–	2	–
Model 1: Context-Free (Section 2.4.1)	0.3	σ	0.5σ	–	–	2	–
Model 2: Context-Dep. (Gradient) (Section 2.4.2.1)	0.3	σ	0.1	0.25	–	2	–
Model 3: Context-Dep. (Discrete) (Section 2.4.2.2)	0.3	σ	–	0.5	–	2	–
Soft-Target Model (Section 4.3)	0.3	σ	0.1	0.25	0.6	2	50

Appendix B: The frequency effect

This material is supplemental to Chapters 2.4.1 and 3.1 of the main text.

The iterative model implies that the frequency effect must arise in the lifetime of the speaker, and only after they have had sufficient exposure to a given (high frequency) category. This may happen very quickly. However, the less time it takes, the more opportunities there will be for lower-frequency categories to "catch up". Therefore, in order to give the best chance to the basic model, I will assume the largest possible time period in which the effect could arise: the age of the experimental population for which frequency effects are found. As the pool of participants for psychology and linguistics experiments is most often university undergraduates, I will take 20 years to be the maximum amount of time necessary to produce a reduction in duration comparable to what has been reported in the literature.

I don't know how many model iterations correspond to 20 years. But I will define the number of productions during this time, for a word of frequency f, as n_f, and the proportion by which it is reduced, as δ_{n_f}, from an initial average duration of $\overline{d_0}$. This period of time will be called an epoch (e).

(B.1) $$\overline{d_{n_f}} = \overline{d_0} - \delta_{n_f}\overline{d_0}$$

To simplify the problem, I will consider a scenario in which there is only a single token belonging to each category, located at the category mean, which is replaced, each time production occurs, by a token reduced by a fixed proportion of the current duration. With this simplification all categories will reduce faster, since it is always the most reduced token that is chosen in production. However, since all measures are comparisons between categories of different frequencies (rather than absolute values), this should not affect the result. Low and high frequency categories are also of exactly the same size token-wise in this simplified scenario, and only update-rate differentiates them. Equalizing low- and high -frequency categories in this way does affect the outcome, as we saw in Section 2.4.1, but it advantages the basic model by ensuring that higher-frequency words are always shorter than lower-frequency ones.

In the simplified scenario, each generation is exponentially more reduced than the last. From Eq (2.3): $x_{o(+n)} = x_o\,(1-\alpha)^n$, I can derive Eq. (B.4), which expresses the duration, after 1 epoch, for a word category of frequency f, and an initial average duration of $\overline{d_0}$. Rewriting Eq. (2.3) in terms of these variables:

(B.2) $$\overline{d_{n_f}} = \overline{d_0}(1-\alpha)^{n_f}$$

Substituting in from Eq. (B.1):

(B.3) $$\overline{d_0} - \delta_{n_f}\overline{d_0} = \overline{d_0}(1-\alpha)^{n_f}$$

And,

(B.4) $$\delta_{n_f} = 1-(1-\alpha)^{n_f}$$

We don't know what the amount of reduction over 1 epoch is. But we do have an idea of the size of the frequency effect: word duration as a function of frequency (log frequency is typically what is plotted in order to make the frequency distribution closer to Normal, see e.g. Gahl et al. 2012). If I assume a linear relation between word duration and log frequency, then for each unit change in log frequency, the difference in word duration should be equal to a constant value (b). Thus, the predicted difference in duration between a low frequency and high frequency word is related to the difference in frequencies by the following formula:

(B.5) $$\frac{\Delta d_e}{\log(f_L)-\log(f_H)} = b$$

If speakers/listeners begin at birth with equal experience of all words – meaning, none – then the differences in duration that accrue over the course of an epoch will be due entirely to the amount of reduction that occurs over that epoch. By the time that one epoch has passed, the higher frequency word of any pair will have reduced more than its counterpart. Assuming that the two words in question are otherwise identical, for our purposes, that they have the same original duration, then the difference in absolute duration at that time will be given by:

(B.6) $$\Delta d_e = \delta_{n_L} - \delta_{n_H}$$

Combining (B.5) and (B.6),

(B.7) $$\delta_{n_L} - \delta_{n_H} = b\left[\log\left(\frac{f_L}{f_H}\right)\right]$$

Substituting in Eq. (B.4):

(B.8) $$1 - (1-\alpha)^{n_L} - [1 - (1-\alpha)^{n_H}] = b\left[\log\left(\frac{f_L}{f_H}\right)\right]$$

Simplifying:

(B.9) $$(1-\alpha)^{n_H} - (1-\alpha)^{n_L} = b\left[\log\left(\frac{f_L}{f_H}\right)\right]$$

The higher the frequency of a given word, the more times it should be produced within a given time period. And if reduction is proportional to the log frequency, with every production resulting in a given amount of reduction, then the number of productions should also be proportional to log frequency.

(B.10) $$n_f = \mathrm{rlog}(f)$$

Substituting (B.10) into (B.9):

(B.11) $$(1-\alpha)^{\mathrm{rlog}(f_H)} - (1-\alpha)^{\mathrm{rlog}(f_L)} = b\left[\log\left(\frac{f_L}{f_H}\right)\right]$$

Assuming that it is possible to find values for α and r that satisfy Eq. (B.11) for all frequencies, the additional reduction that will occur over the lifetime of the speaker can then be determined.

If 1 epoch corresponds to about 20 years, then there will be about 4 over the lifetime of an individual. If I assume a constant rate of production for each category proportional to its frequency, then lifetime (E) average reduction is given by $\delta_{E_f} = 1 - (1-\alpha)^{4n_f}$, which can be rewritten as:

(B.12) $$\delta_{E_f} = 1 - (1-\alpha)^{4\,\mathrm{rlog}(f)}$$

With the necessary constants, I can now determine the difference in reduction between the same two word categories after 4 epochs. If I assume that there exists a floor beyond which words cannot reduce further, then I will need to determine if any words are predicted to reach floor in the lifetime of the speaker, and what effect that will have on the behavior of the frequency dependence – either entirely neutralizing the duration difference between certain words, or decreasing that difference to some extent.

The exact predictions of the linearly biased frequency model will depend on a host of implementational details. As already discussed in the text, the choice of whether lower-frequency categories should have proportionally fewer tokens than higher-frequency categories will affect the outcome. Other parameters that have the potential to alter the outcome include whether or not each individual experience is automatically added to memory – or only a certain minimum number, or some average of recent experience – and how quickly older memories decay, being replaced by new experiences. It may be possible, if unlikely, that at least one set of parameter values exists that will prevent any words reaching floor within the lifetime of the speaker. However, under any parameter settings, all words are predicted to continue reducing over the lifetime of the speaker. This prediction is empirically testable.

Appendix C: Derivation of State Model

This material is supplemental to Section 4.5.1 of the main text.

For the Pure State Model (G), with 2-targets, each sub-category is subject to two forces: entrenchment, and inertia. Under the simplifying assumption that each sub-category can be treated as a Normal distribution with constant variance, the equilibrium locations of the sub-category means can be derived in the following way. At equilibrium the entrenchment force is balanced by the inertial force due to each sub-category's attractor. The location of the sub-category mean is the location at which the displacement that would occur due to the entrenchment force is exactly counteracted by the displacement that would occur due to the inertia force. For the non-biased sub-category this equilibrium occurs under the following conditions:

$$\beta\left(\overline{x_E^{NB}} - N\right) = \varepsilon\left(\overline{x_E} - \overline{x_E^{NB}}\right) \tag{C.1}$$

For the biased sub-category, equilibrium occurs when:

$$\alpha\left(\overline{x_E^{B}} - L\right) = \varepsilon\left(\overline{x_E} - \overline{x_E^{B}}\right) \tag{C.2}$$

Because the entrenchment force depends on the global mean, so too do the two equilibrium equations. In turn, the global mean can be expressed as a function of the sub-category means (where the proportion of biased tokens is given by p):

$$\overline{x_E} = (1-p)\overline{x_E^{NB}} + p\overline{x_E^{B}} \tag{C.3}$$

With three equations, we can solve for the three distribution means. Solving for $\overline{x_E^{NB}}$ in Eq. (C.1):

$$\overline{x_E^{NB}} = \frac{\beta N + \varepsilon\overline{x_E}}{\beta + \varepsilon} \tag{C.4}$$

Solving for $\overline{x_E^B}$ in Eq. (C.2):

$$\overline{x_E^B} = \frac{\alpha L + \varepsilon \overline{x_E}}{\alpha + \varepsilon} \tag{C.5}$$

Substituting these two values into Eq. (C.3):

$$\overline{x_E} = (1-p)\frac{\beta N + \varepsilon \overline{x_E}}{\beta + \varepsilon} + p\frac{\alpha L + \varepsilon \overline{x_E}}{\alpha + \varepsilon} \tag{C.6}$$

Solving for $\overline{x_E}$ as a function of p, and collecting terms:

$$\overline{x_E} = \frac{(1-p)\beta N}{\beta + \varepsilon} + \frac{(1-p)\varepsilon \overline{x_E}}{\beta + \varepsilon} + \frac{p\alpha L}{\alpha + \varepsilon} + \frac{p\varepsilon \overline{x_E}}{\alpha + \varepsilon} \tag{C.7}$$

$$\overline{x_E} - \frac{(1-p)\varepsilon \overline{x_E}}{\beta + \varepsilon} - \frac{p\varepsilon \overline{x_E}}{\alpha + \varepsilon} = \frac{(1-p)\beta N}{\beta + \varepsilon} + \frac{p\alpha L}{\alpha + \varepsilon} \tag{C.8}$$

$$\frac{\overline{x_E}(\beta + \varepsilon)(\alpha + \varepsilon) - (\alpha + \varepsilon)(1-p)\varepsilon \overline{x_E} - (\beta + \varepsilon)p\varepsilon \overline{x_E}}{(\beta + \varepsilon)(\alpha + \varepsilon)} = \frac{(1-p)\beta N}{\beta + \varepsilon} + \frac{p\alpha L}{\alpha + \varepsilon} \tag{C.9}$$

$$\frac{\overline{x_E}(\beta + \varepsilon)(\alpha + \varepsilon) - (\alpha + \varepsilon)(1-p)\varepsilon \overline{x_E} - (\beta + \varepsilon)p\varepsilon \overline{x_E}}{(\beta + \varepsilon)(\alpha + \varepsilon)} = \frac{(1-p)\beta N(\alpha + \varepsilon) + p\alpha L(\beta + \varepsilon)}{(\alpha + \varepsilon)(\beta + \varepsilon)} \tag{C.10}$$

$$\overline{x_E}\left[(\beta + \varepsilon)(\alpha + \varepsilon) - (\alpha + \varepsilon)(1-p)\varepsilon - (\beta + \varepsilon)p\varepsilon\right] = (1-p)\beta N(\alpha + \varepsilon) + p\alpha L(\beta + \varepsilon) \tag{C.11}$$

$$\overline{x_E} = \frac{(1-p)\beta N(\alpha + \varepsilon) + p\alpha L(\beta + \varepsilon)}{(\beta + \varepsilon)(\alpha + \varepsilon) - (\alpha + \varepsilon)(1-p)\varepsilon - (\beta + \varepsilon)p\varepsilon} \tag{C.12}$$

Eq. (C.12) is a complex function of $\alpha, \beta, \varepsilon, N, L$, and p, the derivative of which is not trivially calculated. For known values of $\alpha, \beta, \varepsilon, N$, and L , $\overline{x_E}(p)$ can be determined exactly. The general behavior of this function, however, can be understood via the following chain of reasoning.

For a given $p = p_i$ (for $p_i < 1$), the equilibrium location of the global mean can be found using Eq. (C.12). Now imagine that p increases from p_i to p_j. This will result in the global mean moving closer to the biased sub-category (Eq. (C.3)). A change in the global mean will cause a change in the entrenchment force for both sub-categories. It will increase for the non-biased sub-category, which is now farther from the global mean; and it will decrease in exactly the same degree for the biased sub-category, which is now closer to the global mean.

Because inertia does not depend on p, the lefthand sides of Eqs. (C.1) and (C.2) will remain constant. Thus, the non-biased sub-category will shift in the direction of the mean – rightward – as a result of the increase in p. The decrease in the entrenchment force on the biased sub-category, conversely, will cause a shift away from the mean, and towards the attractor at L. This is also a rightward shift, however. The net effect will be to perturb the sub-categories from their former equilibrium locations to points farther to the right, and closer to L. As p increases, $\overline{x_E}$ will always increase (as long as both sub-categories are located between N and L).

The distance between the means of the two sub-categories can also be written as a function of p. Once equilibrium has been reached, the separation can be derived from Eqs. (C.1) and (C.2):

$$\Delta\overline{x_E} \equiv \overline{x_E^B} - \overline{x_E^{NB}} = \frac{\alpha L + \varepsilon\overline{x_E}}{\alpha + \varepsilon} - \frac{\beta N + \varepsilon\overline{x_E}}{\beta + \varepsilon} \tag{C.13}$$

Collecting terms and simplifying:

$$= \frac{\alpha L}{\alpha + \varepsilon} - \frac{\beta N}{\beta + \varepsilon} + \frac{\varepsilon\overline{x_E}}{\alpha + \varepsilon} - \frac{\varepsilon\overline{x_E}}{\beta + \varepsilon} \tag{C.14}$$

$$= \frac{\alpha L}{\alpha + \varepsilon} - \frac{\beta N}{\beta + \varepsilon} + \varepsilon\overline{x_E}\left[\frac{1}{\alpha + \varepsilon} - \frac{1}{\beta + \varepsilon}\right] \tag{C.15}$$

The change in sub-category separation as a function of changing p is thus given by:

$$\frac{\partial \Delta \overline{x_E}}{\partial p} = \frac{\partial \overline{x_E}}{\partial p}\varepsilon\left[\frac{1}{\alpha+\varepsilon} - \frac{1}{\beta+\varepsilon}\right] \tag{C.16}$$

In order to determine $\frac{\partial \Delta \overline{x_E}}{\partial p}$, we must be able to calculate $\frac{\partial \overline{x_E}}{\partial p}$. For the special case in which all forces have the same strength ($\alpha = \beta = \varepsilon$), it is straightforward to calculate the derivative of Eq. (C.12):

$$\overline{x_E} = \frac{2\alpha^2 N + p(2\alpha^2 L - 2\alpha^2 N)}{4\alpha^2 - 2\alpha^2} \tag{C.17}$$

Collecting terms and simplifying:

$$\overline{x_E} = \frac{2\alpha^2[N + pL - pN]}{2\alpha^2[2-1]} \tag{C.18}$$

$$\overline{x_E} = N + p(L - N) \tag{C.19}$$

This gives the expected behavior; for $p = 0$, there is only the non-biased distribution, which is stable at N, and for $p = 1$, there is only the biased distribution, which is stable at L. For equal numbers of biased and non-biased variants, each sub-category stabilizes at the same distance from its attractor, and the global mean is halfway between the two. The change in the global category mean as a function of p is a positive, fixed value: $L - N$, the derivative of (C.19). Plugging this value for $\partial \overline{x_E}/\partial p$ into Eq. (C.16) gives:

$$\frac{\partial \Delta \overline{x_E}}{\partial p} = (L - N)\alpha\left[\frac{1}{2\alpha} - \frac{1}{2\alpha}\right] = 0 \tag{C.20}$$

Thus, while the overall category mean gets larger as p increases, the separation between the categories remains constant.

In the general case, the separation between the two sub-categories will show different behavior for different parameter values. Because $\partial \overline{x_E}/\partial p > 0$, the sign of $\partial \Delta \overline{x_E}/\partial p$ depends on the $\varepsilon[1/(\alpha+\varepsilon) - 1/(\beta+\varepsilon)]$ term. When $\alpha < \beta$, the separation increases with increasing p. This follows from the fact that $\partial \Delta \overline{x_E}/\partial p$ is positive only when $\varepsilon[1/(\alpha+\varepsilon) - 1/(\beta+\varepsilon)] > 0$. For $\varepsilon[1/(\alpha+\varepsilon) - 1/(\beta+\varepsilon)]$ to be greater than zero it must be the case that $1/(\alpha+\varepsilon) > 1/(\beta+\varepsilon)$. This, in turn, requires that $\alpha < \beta$. By the same reasoning, the separation decreases as a function of increasing p when $\alpha > \beta$. Finally, the separation remains constant when $\alpha = \beta$, because this entails that $\varepsilon[1/(\alpha + \varepsilon) - 1/(\beta + \varepsilon)] = 0$, verifying the result in Eq. (C.20).

Appendix D: Derivation of Process Model

This material is supplemental to Section 4.5.2 of the main text.

For the Pure Process Model, there is a single category, and all tokens are subject to the same inertial force, in proportion to their distance from the single attractor at N. Additionally, a proportion p of randomly selected tokens undergo a lengthening process, moving away from the rest of the distribution during production. The simplifying assumption, that each sub-distribution can be treated as a Normal distribution with constant variance, is adopted. To derive the model behavior I will look at the contribution of the different forces in stages. This derivation references the stages depicted in Figure 4.3.

First I apply the lengthening process, at time t, to tokens drawn from a distribution with a global mean of $\overline{x_t}$. These tokens are simultaneously subjected to an inertial force. Eq. (D.1) gives the mean of the biased sub-distribution at time t,

(D.1) $$\overline{x_t^B}' = \overline{x_t}(1+\alpha) + \beta(N - \overline{x_t})$$

and Eq. (D.2) gives the means of the non-biased sub-distribution at time t.

(D.2) $$\overline{x_t^{NB}}' = \overline{x_t} + \beta(N - \overline{x_t})$$

On average, a proportion p of the distribution will be lengthened, thus the location of the global mean, after lengthening and inertia apply, can be expressed as

(D.3) $$\overline{x_t}' = (1-p)\overline{x_t^{NB}}' + p\overline{x_t^B}'$$

Entrenchment must also be applied in order to determine the final outcome, but entrenchment does not affect the location of the global mean, only the locations of the sub-distribution means, and their separation. To see this, I can compare the global mean before and after entrenchment applies. After entrenchment, the means of each sub-distribution are given by:

(D.4) $$\overline{x_t^B}'' = \overline{x_t^B}' - \varepsilon\left(\overline{x_t}' - \overline{x_t^B}'\right)$$

(D.5) $$\overline{x_t^{NB}}'' = \overline{x_t^{NB}}' - \varepsilon\left(\overline{x_t}' - \overline{x_t^{NB}}'\right)$$

Substituting into Eq. (D.3), gives

(D.6) $$\overline{x_t}'' = (1-p)\left[\overline{x_t^{NB}}' - \varepsilon\left(\overline{x_t}' - \overline{x_t^{NB}}'\right)\right] + p\left[\overline{x_t^B}' - \varepsilon\left(\overline{x_t}' - \overline{x_t^B}'\right)\right]$$

Simplifying and collecting terms:

(D.7) $$= \overline{x_t}' - \varepsilon(1-p)\left(\overline{x_t}' - \overline{x_t^{NB}}'\right) - p\varepsilon\left(\overline{x_t}' - \overline{x_t^B}'\right)$$

(D.8) $$= \overline{x_t}' + \varepsilon(1-p)\overline{x_t^{NB}}' - [\varepsilon(1-p) + p\varepsilon]\,\overline{x_t}' + p\varepsilon\overline{x_t^B}'$$

(D.9) $$= \overline{x_t}' - \varepsilon\overline{x_t}' + \varepsilon\left[(1-p)\overline{x_t^{NB}}' + p\overline{x_t^B}'\right]$$

The term $(1-p)\overline{x_t^{NB}}' + p\overline{x_t^B}'$ is equivalent to $\overline{x_t}'$ by Eq. (D.3). Therefore

(D.10) $$\overline{x_t}'' = \overline{x_t}' - \varepsilon\overline{x_t}' + \varepsilon\overline{x_t}' = \overline{x_t}'$$

Because it does not depend on entrenchment, the global mean at equilibrium can be determined directly from (D.1) and (D.2). Equilibrium occurs when the two sub-distributions are also at equilibrium, and the global mean stops changing: $\overline{x_E} = \overline{x_E}'$, $\overline{x_E^{NB}}' = \overline{x_E^{NB}}$, and $\overline{x_E^B}' = \overline{x_E^B}$. Therefore,

(D.11) $$\overline{x_E} = (1-p)\overline{x_E^{NB}}' + p\overline{x_E^B}'$$

Substituting in Eqs. (D.1) and (D.2):

(D.12) $$\overline{x_E} = [\overline{x_E} + \beta(N - \overline{x_E})] - p[\overline{x_E} + \beta(N - \overline{x_E})] + p[\overline{x_E} + \overline{x_E}\alpha + \beta(N - \overline{x_E})]$$

Simplifying and collecting terms:

$$\text{(D.13)} \quad \overline{x_E} = \overline{x_E} + \beta(N - \overline{x_E}) + p\overline{x_E}\alpha - p[\overline{x_E} + \beta(N - \overline{x_E})] + p[\overline{x_E} - \beta(N - \overline{x_E})]$$

$$\overline{x_E} = \overline{x_E} + \beta(N - \overline{x_E}) + p\overline{x_E}\alpha \tag{D.14}$$

$$\overline{x_E} = \overline{x_E}(1 - \beta + p\alpha) + \beta N \tag{D.15}$$

$$\overline{x_E}(1 - 1 + \beta - p\alpha) = \beta N \tag{D.16}$$

$$\overline{x_E} = \frac{\beta N}{\beta - p\alpha} \tag{D.17}$$

For the case when $p\alpha < \beta$, the denominator in (D.17) is positive. As p increases (but $p\alpha$ remains smaller than β), the denominator decreases, and the global mean increases. As $p\alpha$ approaches β, the global mean goes to infinity; lengthening is unbounded. For $p\alpha > \beta$ the only stable point is negative, and thus there is no well-defined equilibrium. The PROCESS model is thus only stable if the lengthening strength is not too great, and the percentage of biasing contexts is not too large.

To calculate the dependence of the sub-distribution separation on p, the effect of entrenchment must be included. The equilibrium separation is defined as:

$$\Delta\overline{x_E}'' \equiv \overline{x_E^B}'' - \overline{x_E^{NB}}'' \tag{D.18}$$

And

$$\overline{x_E^B}'' = \overline{x_E^B}' + \varepsilon\left(\overline{x_E}' - \overline{x_E^B}'\right) \tag{D.19}$$

$$\overline{x_E^{NB}}'' = \overline{x_E^{NB}}' + \varepsilon\left(\overline{x_E}' - \overline{x_E^{NB}}'\right) \tag{D.20}$$

Therefore,

(D.21) $$\overline{x_E^B}'' - \overline{x_E^{NB}}'' = \overline{x_E^B}' - \overline{x_E^{NB}}' + \varepsilon\left(\overline{x_E}' - \overline{x_E^B}'\right) - \varepsilon\left(\overline{x_E}' - \overline{x_E^{NB}}'\right)$$

Collecting terms:

(D.22) $$= \overline{x_E^B}' - \overline{x_E^{NB}}' - \varepsilon\left(\overline{x_E^B}' - \overline{x_E^{NB}}'\right)$$

and

(D.23) $$\Delta\overline{x_E}'' = (1-\varepsilon)\left(\overline{x_E^B}' - \overline{x_E^{NB}}'\right)$$

The observed separation at equilibrium depends on the separation due to prior model forces. From Eqs. (D.1) and (D.2),

(D.24) $$\overline{x_E^B}' - \overline{x_E^{NB}}' = \overline{x_E}(1+\alpha) + \beta(N - \overline{x_E}) - [\overline{x_E} + \beta(N - \overline{x_E})]$$

This reduces to $\alpha\overline{x_E}$. Note that this is exactly the amount that biased tokens are shifted away from the mean at equilibrium. Because this is a PROCESS model, the separation created by the lengthening bias only exists transiently, and it is not possible for any specific subset of tokens to continue to increase their separation from the rest of the distribution. Therefore, the prior separation between the sub-distribution means is always given by the lengthening bias applied to that mean. And the total separation, by

(D.25) $$\Delta\overline{x_E} = (1-\epsilon)(\alpha\overline{x_E}).$$

In the stable parameter range, where $\overline{x_E}$ increases as p increases, the separation of the sub-distributions also increases, but more slowly, by a factor of $\alpha(1-\epsilon)$.

Appendix E: Nasalization model parameters

The following parameters were identical for the two models:

- The entrenchment strength is set to $\varepsilon = 0.2$
- The production error on each articulatory dimension is drawn from the distribution $\mathcal{N}\left(0, 0.25\sigma_{x^Z}\right)$, where σ_{x^Z} indicates the standard deviation of the current distribution of stored tokens on dimension x^Z
- Speaking Rate:
  - Expansion force (E) is a random variable distributed according to $\mathcal{N}(0, 0.25)$.
  - The speaking rate transformation lengthens or shortens a given duration parameter, according to the following dependence on E:

  (E.1)
  $$x_i^{O'} = \frac{2x_i^O}{(1 + e^{k_O E})}$$

  (E.2)
  $$x_i^{V'} = \frac{2x_i^V}{(1 + e^{-k_V E})}$$

  (E.3)
  $$x_i^{N'} = \frac{2x_i^N}{(1 + e^{-k_N E})}$$

  For these simulations all gestures are set to the same elasticity ($k_O = k_N = k_V = 1$).

- Model outputs are reported after 10,000 iterations
- x_i^O is never allowed to fall below 0, or to exceed the shorter of the two values (x_i^N, x_i^V)

- The duration of x_i^V is never allowed to fall below 50 ms, or to exceed 600 ms
- The duration of x_i^N is never allowed to fall below 25 ms, or to exceed 500 ms

E.1 No-Phoneme Model

The fluency attractor affects overlap duration according to the following formula:

$$x_i^{O'} = x_i^O + \beta(T - x_i^O) \tag{E.4}$$

The target overlap duration for these simulations is set at $T = x_i^N$. β parameterizes frequency on a scale between 0 and 1.

E.2 Multiple-Parse Model

- Resting activation acts as a perturbation to the expansion force, E. The mean of the expansion function is shifted $1/4$ of a standard deviation for each unit of f, where f parameterizes frequency:

  $$\overline{E}' = \overline{E} - f(0.25\sigma_E)$$

- The overlap duration for Analysis 2 tokens is a random variable distributed according to $\mathcal{N}\left(0.25\overline{x^N}, \sigma_{x^N}\right)$
- The probability of Analysis 1 is given by:

  $$P(a = 1) = Ae^{-b(1-Q)} - C \tag{E.5}$$

  where $Q = x_i^O / x_i^N$. For all simulations, the constants are set to: $A = 1$, $b = 2$, and $C = 0$.

References

Archangeli, Diana. 1988. Aspects of underspecification theory. *Phonology* 5(2). 183–207. DOI:10.1017/S0952675700002268

Aylett, Matthew & Alice Turk. 2004. The smooth signal redundancy hypothesis: A functional explanation for relationships between redundancy, prosodic prominence, and duration in spontaneous speech. *Language and Speech* 47(1). 31–56. DOI:10.1177/00238309040470010201

Baayen, Harald. 1993. On frequency, transparency and productivity. In Geert Booij & Jaap van Marle (eds.), *Yearbook of morphology 1992*, 181–208. Springer, Dordrecht. DOI:10.1007/978-94-017-3710-4_7

Baayen, Harald, Ton Dijkstra & Robert Schreuder. 1997. Singulars and plurals in Dutch: Evidence for a parallel dual-route model. *Journal of Memory and Language* 37(1). 94–117. DOI:10.1006/jmla.1997.2509

Baese-Berk, Melissa & Matthew Goldrick. 2009. Mechanisms of interaction in speech production. *Language and Cognitive Processes* 24(4). 527–554. DOI:10.1080/01690960802299378

Baker, Adam, Diana Archangeli & Jeff Mielke. 2011. Variability in American English s-retraction suggests a solution to the actuation problem. *Language Variation and Change* 23(3). 347–374. DOI:10.1017/S0954394511000135

Balota, David A. & James I. Chumbley. 1985. The locus of word-frequency effects in the pronunciation task: Lexical access and/or production? *Journal of Memory and Language* 24(1). 89–106. DOI:10.1016/0749-596X(85)90017-8

Bates, Elizabeth & Judith C. Goodman. 1997. On the inseparability of grammar and the lexicon: Evidence from acquisition, aphasia and real-time processing. *Language and Cognitive Processes* 12(5–6). 507–584. DOI:10.1080/016909697386628

Baxter, Gareth J., Richard A. Blythe, William Croft & Alan J. McKane. 2006. Utterance selection model of language change. *Physical Review E* 73(4) (Article 046118). DOI:10.1103/PhysRevE.73.046118

Beckman, Jill, Pétur Helgason, Bob McMurray & Catherine Ringen. 2011. Rate effects on Swedish VOT: Evidence for phonological overspecification. *Journal of Phonetics* 39(1). 39–49. DOI:10.1016/j.wocn.2010.11.001

Beckman, Mary E. & Jan Edwards. 2000. The ontogeny of phonological categories and the primacy of lexical learning in linguistic development. *Child Development* 71(1). 240–249. DOI:10.1111/1467-8624.00139

Beddor, Patrice Speeter. 2009. A coarticulatory path to sound change. *Language* 85(4). 785–821. DOI:10.1353/lan.0.0165

Belasco, Simon. 1958. Variations in vowel duration: Phonemically or phonetically conditioned? *The Journal of the Acoustical Society of America* 30(11). 1049–1050. DOI:10.1121/1.1909457

Bell-Berti, Fredericka. 1993. Understanding velic motor control: Studies of segmental context. In Marie Huffman & Rena Krakow (eds.), *Nasals, nasalization, and the velum* (Phonetics and Phonology 5), 63–85. San Diego: Academic Press. DOI:10.1016/B978-0-12-360380-7.50007-7

Bell, Alan, Daniel Jurafsky, Eric Fosler-Lussier, Cynthia Girand, Michelle Gregory & Daniel Gildea. 2003. Effects of disfluencies, predictability and utterance position on word form variation in English conversation. *Journal of the Acoustical Society of America* 113(2). 1001–1024. DOI:10.1121/1.1534836

Blevins, Juliette. 2004. *Evolutionary phonology: The emergence of sound patterns.* New York: Cambridge University Press.

Blevins, Juliette & Andrew Wedel. 2009. Inhibited sound change: An evolutionary approach to lexical competition. *Diachronica* 26(2). 143–183. DOI:doi:10.1075/dia.26.2.01ble

Browman, Catherine P. & Louis M. Goldstein. 1988. Some notes on syllable structure in articulatory phonology. *Phonetica* 45(2–4). 140–155. DOI:10.1159/000261823

Browman, Catherine P. & Louis M. Goldstein. 1990. Tiers in articulatory phonology, with some implications for casual speech. In John Kingston & Mary E. Beckman (eds.), *Papers in laboratory phonology I: Between the grammar and the physics of speech*, 341–376. Cambridge: Cambridge University Press.

Brown, Esther L. & William D. Raymond. 2012. How discourse context shapes the lexicon: Explaining the distribution of Spanish f- / h- words. *Diachronica* 29(2). 139–162. DOI:10.1075/dia.29.2.02bro

Burani, Cristina & Alfonso Caramazza. 1987. Representation and processing of derived words. *Language and Cognitive Processes* 2(3–4). 217–227.

Bybee, Joan. 2001. *Phonology and language use.* Cambridge: Cambridge University Press. DOI:10.1017/CBO9780511612886

Bybee, Joan. 2002. Word frequency and context of use in the lexical diffusion of phonetically conditioned sound change. *Language Variation and Change* 14(3). 261–290. DOI:10.1017/S0954394502143018

Bybee, Joan. 2003. Mechanisms of change in grammaticization: The role of frequency. In Brian D. Joseph & Richard D. Janda (eds.), *The handbook of historical linguistics*, 602–623. London: Blackwell. DOI:10.1002/9780470756393.ch19

Bybee, Joan. 2006. From usage to grammar: The mind's response to repetition. *Language* 82(4). 711–733.

Byrd, Dani. 1996. Influences on articulatory timing in consonant sequences. *Journal of Phonetics* 24(2). 209–244. DOI:10.1006/jpho.1996.0012

Caramazza, Alfonso, Alessandro Laudanna & Cristina Romani. 1988. Lexical access and inflectional morphology. *Cognition* 28(3). 297–332. DOI:10.1016/0010-0277(88)90017-0

Chang, Steve, Madelain C. Plauche & John J. Ohala. 2001. Markedness and consonant confusion asymmetries. In Elizabeth Hume & Keith Johnson (eds.), *The role of speech perception in phonology*, 79–101. Leiden: Brill.

Chen, Matthew. 1970. Vowel length variation as a function of the voicing of the consonant environment. *Phonetica* 22(3). 129–159. DOI:10.1159/000259312

Cho, Taehong. 2001. Effects of morpheme boundaries on intergestural timing: Evidence from Korean. *Phonetica* 58(3). 129–162. DOI:10.1159/000056196

Choi, John D. 1995. An acoustic-phonetic underspecification account of Marshallese vowel allophony. *Journal of Phonetics* 23(3). 323–347. DOI:10.1016/S0095-4470(95)80164-2

Chomsky, Noam & Morris Halle. 1968. *The sound pattern of English.* New York City: Harper & Row.

Cohn, Abigail. 1990. *Phonetic and phonological Rules of nasalization.* UCLA dissertation.

Davis, Matthew H. & Ingrid S. Johnsrude. 2007. Hearing speech sounds: Top-down influences on the interface between audition and speech perception. *Hearing Research* 229(1–2). 132–147. DOI:10.1016/j.heares.2007.01.014

de Boer, Bart. 2000. Emergence of vowel systems through self-organisation. *AI Communications* 13(1). 27–39.

Delattre, Pierre. 1962. Some factors of vowel duration and their cross-linguistic validity. *The Journal of the Acoustical Society of America* 34(8). 1141–1143. DOI:10.1121/1.1918268

Dell, Gary. 1986. A spreading activation theory of retrieval in language production. *Psychological Review* 93(3). 282–321. DOI:10.1037/0033-295X.93.3.283

Dillon, Brian, Ewan Dunbar & William Idsardi. 2013. A single-stage approach to learning phonological categories: Insights from Inuktitut. *Cognitive Science* 37(2). 344–377. DOI:10.1111/cogs.12008

Docherty, Gerard J. & Paul Foulkes. 2014. An evaluation of usage-based approaches to the modelling of sociophonetic variability. *Lingua* 142. 42–56. DOI:10.1016/j.lingua.2013.01.011

Ettlinger, Marc. 2007. An exemplar-based model of chain shifts. In *Proceedings of the 16th international congress of the phonetic science*, 685–688.

Fagyal, Zsuzsanna, Samarth Swarup, Anna Maria Escobar, Les Gasser & Kiran Lakkaraju. 2010. Centers and peripheries: Network roles in language change. *Lingua* 120(8). 2061–2079. DOI:10.1016/j.lingua.2010.02.001

Feldman, Naomi, Thomas Griffiths & James Morgan. 2009. Learning phonetic categories by learning a lexicon. *Proceedings of the Annual Meeting of the Cognitive Science Society* 31(31). 2208–2213.

Frauenfelder, Uli H. & Robert Schreuder. 1992. Constraining psycholinguistic models of morphological processing and representation: The role of productivity. In Gert Booij & Jaap van Marle (eds.), *Yearbook of morphology 1991*, 165–183. Dordrecht: Springer.

Gahl, Susanne. 2008. Time and thyme are not homophones: The effect of lemma frequency on word durations in spontaneous speech. *Language* 84(3). 474–496. DOI:10.1353/lan.0.0035

Gahl, Susanne, Yao Yao & Keith Johnson. 2012. Why reduce? Phonological neighborhood density and phonetic reduction in spontaneous speech. *Journal of Memory and Language* 66(4). 789–806. DOI:10.1016/j.jml.2011.11.006

Ganong, William F. 1980. Phonetic categorization in auditory word perception. *Journal of Experimental Psychology: Human Perception and Performance* 6(1). 110–125.

Garrett, Andrew & Keith Johnson. 2013. Phonetic bias in sound change. In Alan Yu (ed.), *Origins of sound change: Approaches to phonologization*, 51–97. Oxford: Oxford University Press.

Gaskell, M. Gareth & William D. Marslen-Wilson. 1996. Phonological variation and inference in lexical access. *Journal of Experimental Psychology: Human Perception and Performance* 22(1). 144–158. DOI:10.1037/0096-1523.22.1.144

Gimson, Alfred Charles. 1970. *An introduction to the pronunciation of English*. London: Hodder Arnold.

Goldinger, Stephen D. 1996. Words and voices: Episodic traces in spoken word identification and recognition memory. *Journal of Experimental Psychology: Learning, Memory and Cognition* 22(5). 1166–1183.

Goldsmith, John & Aris Xanthos. 2009. Learning phonological categories. *Language* 85(1). 4–38.

Gow, David. 2003. Feature parsing: Feature cue mapping in spoken word recognition. *Attention, Perception, & Psychophysics* 65 (4). 575–590.

Guion, Susan G. 1998. The role of perception in the sound change of velar palatalization. *Phonetica* 55. 18–52.

Guy, Gregory R. 2008. Variationist approaches to phonological change. In Brian D. Joseph & Richard D. Janda (eds.), *The handbook of historical linguistics*, 369–400. Oxford: Oxford, UK: Blackwell Publishing Ltd. DOI:10.1002/9780470756393.ch8

Hajek, John. 1997. *Universals of sound change in nasalization*. London: Wiley-Blackwell.

Hajek, John & Shinji Maeda. 2000. Investigation universals of sound change: The effect of vowel height and duration on the development of distinctive nasalization. In B. Broe Michael & Janet B. Pierrehumber (eds.), *Papers in laboratory phonology v: acquisition and the lexicon*, 52–69. Cambridge University Press.

Hardcastle, William J. 1985. Some phonetic and syntactic constraints on lingual coarticulation in stop consonant sequences. *Speech Communication* 4. 247–263.

Hintzman, Douglas L. 1984. MINERVA 2: A simulation model of human memory. *Behavior Research Methods, Instruments, & Computers* 16(2). 96–101.

Hooper, Joan B. 1976. Word frequency in lexical diffusion and the source of morphophonological change. In William Christie (ed.), *Current progress in historical linguistics*, 96–105. Amsterdam: North Holland.

Howes, Davis H. & Richard L. Solomon. 1951. Visual duration threshold as a function of word-probability. *Journal of Experimental Psychology* 41(6). 401–410.

Hyman, Larry M. 1975. Nasal states and nasal processes. In Charles A. Ferguson, Larry M. Hyman & John J. Ohala (eds.), *Nasalfest: Papers from a symposium on nasals and nasalization*, 249–264. Stanford University: Standford: Language Universals Project.

Janda, Richard D. 2008. Phonologization as the start of dephoneticization or, on sound change and its aftermath: Of extension, generalization, lexicalization, and morphologization. In Brian D. Joseph & Richard D. Janda (eds.), *The handbook of historical linguistics*, 401–422. Oxford, UK: Blackwell. DOI:10.1002/9780470756393.ch9

Janda, Richard D. & Brian D. Joseph. 2003. Reconsidering the canons of sound-change: Towards a "big bang" theory. In Barry J. Blake & Kate Burridge (eds.), *Selected Papers from the 15th International Conference on Historical Linguistics*, 205–219. Amsterdam: John Benjamins Publishing Co.

Javkin, Hector. 1977. *Phonetic universals and phonological change*. U.C. Berkeley dissertation.

Johnson, Keith. 1997. Speech perception without speaker normalization: An exemplar model. In Keith Johnson & John W. Mullennix (eds.), *Talker variability in speech processing*, 145–165. San Diego: Academic Press.

Kawasaki, Haruko. 1978. The perceived nasality of vowels with gradual attenuation of adjacent nasal consonants. *The Journal of the Acoustical Society of America* 64(S1). S19. DOI:doi.org/10.1121/1.2004085

Keating, Patricia A. 1985. Universal phonetics and the organization of grammars. In Victoria A. Fromkin (ed.), *Phonetic linguistics: Essays in honor of Peter Ladefoged*, 115–132. Orlando: Academic Press.

Keating, Patricia A. & Aditi Lahiri. 1993. Fronted velars, palatalized velars, and palatals. *Phonetica* 50 (2). 73–101. DOI:10.1159/000261928

Kirby, James P. 2014. Incipient tonogenesis in Phnom Penh Khmer: Computational studies. *Laboratory Phonology* 5(1). 195–230. DOI:10.1515/lp-2014-0008

Klatt, Dennis H. 1976. Linguistic uses of segmental duration in English: Acoustic and perceptual evidence. *The Journal of the Acoustical Society of America* 59(5). 1208–1221. DOI:10.1121/1.380986

Kluender, Keith R., Randy L. Diehl & Beverly A. Wright. 1988. Vowel-length differences before voiced and voiceless consonants: An auditory explanation. *Journal of Phonetics* 16 (2). 153–169.

Krakow, Rena A., Patrice S. Beddor, Louis M. Goldstein & Carol A. Fowler. 1988. Coarticulatory influences on the perceived height of nasal vowels. *The Journal of the Acoustical Society of America* 83(3). 1146–1158. DOI:10.1121/1.396059

Levelt, Willem J.M., Ardi Roelofs & Antje S. Meyer. 1999. A theory of lexical access in speech production. *Behavioral and Brain Sciences* 22(1). 1–38.

Liberman, Alvin M., Franklin S. Cooper, Donald P. Shankweiler & Michael Studdert-Kennedy. 1967. Perception of the speech code. *Psychological Review* 74(6). 431–461. DOI:10.1037/h0020279

Liberman, Alvin M., Pierre C. Delattre, Franklin S. Cooper & Louis J. Gerstman. 1954. The role of consonant-vowel transitions in the perception of the stop and nasal consonants. *Psychological Monographs: General and Applied* 68(8). 1.

Lindblom, Björn. 1990. Explaining phonetic variation: A sketch of the H and H theory. In William J. Hardcastle & Alain Marchal (eds.), *Speech production and speech modelling*, 403–439. Dordrecht: Kluwer. DOI:10.1007/978-94-009-2037-8_16

Lindblom, Björn. 1963. Spectrographic study of vowel reduction. *Journal of the Acoustical Society of America* 35. 1773–1781. DOI:10.1121/1.1918816

Lisker, Leigh. 1957. Closure duration and the intervocalic voiced-voiceless distinction in English. *Language* 33(1). 42–49.

Lisker, Leigh. 1974. On "explaining" vowel duration variation. *Glossa* 8(2). 233–246.

Luce, Paul A. 1986. *Neighborhoods of words in the mental lexicon. Research on speech perception. Technical report No. 6.* Tech. rep. Indiana University. 1–91.

Malécot, André. 1960. Vowel nasality as a distinctive feature in American English. *Language* 32(1) (2). 222–229. DOI:10.2307/410987

Marr, David. 1982. *Vision: A computational investigation into the human representation and processing of visual information.* Henry Holt & Co. 2–46. DOI:10.7551/mitpress/9780262514620.001.0001

Marslen-Wilson, William D. 1990. Activation, competition, and frequency in lexical access. In G. T. M. Altmann (ed.), *Cognitive models of speech processing: Psycholinguistic and computational perspectives*, 148–172. Cambridge, MA: MIT Press.

Martinet, André. 1955. *Economie des changements phonetiques.* Bern: Francke.

McClelland, James L. & David E. Rumelhart. 1981. An interactive activation model of context effects in letter perception: I. An account of basic findings. *Psychological Review* 88(5). 375–407. DOI:10.1037/0033-295X.88.5.375

McMurray, Bob & Allard Jongman. 2011. What information is necessary for speech categorization? Harnessing variability in the speech signal by integrating cues computed relative to expectations. *Psychological Review* 118(2). 219–246. DOI:10.1037/a0022325

Mielke, Jeff. 2008. *The emergence of distinctive features.* Oxford: Oxford University Press.

Milroy, James & Lesley Milroy. 1985. Linguistic change, social network and speaker innovation. *Journal of Linguistics* 21(2). 339–384. DOI:10.1017/S0022226700010306

Moreton, Elliott. 2004. Realization of the English postvocalic [voice] contrast in F1 and F2. *Journal of Phonetics* 32(1). 1–33. DOI:10.1016/s0095-4470(03)00004-4

Morley, Rebecca L. 2014. Implications of an exemplar-theoretic model of phoneme genesis: A velar palatalization case study. *Language and Speech* 57(1). 3–41. DOI:10.1177/0023830913478926

Morley, Rebecca L. & Bridget Smith. in prep. An explanation for the voicing effect: Limits on the expandibility of lenis stops in English.

Munson, Benjamin & Nancy Pearl Solomon. 2004. The effect of phonological neighborhood density on vowel articulation. *Journal of Speech, Language, and Hearing Research* 47. 1048–1058.

Niyogi, Partha & Robert C. Berwick. 1997. A dynamical systems model for language change. *Complex Systems* 11. 161–204.

Nosofsky, Robert M. 1988. Exemplar-based accounts of relations between classification, recognition, and typicality. *Journal of Experimental Psychology: Learning, Memory, and Cognition* 14(4). 700–708. DOI:10.1037/0278-7393.14.4.700

Nowak, Martin A., Natalia L. Komarova & Partha Niyogi. 2001. Evolution of Universal Grammar. *Science* 291(5501). 114–118. DOI:10.1126/science.291.5501.114

Ohala, John J. 1981a. Articulatory constraints on the cognitive representation of speech. *Advances in Psychology* 7. 111–122. DOI:10.1016/S0166-4115(08)60183-1

Ohala, John J. 1981b. The listener as a source of sound change. In C. S. Masek, R. A. Hendrick & M. F. Miller (eds.), *Parasession on language and behavior*, 178–203. Chicago: Chicago Linguistics Society.

Ohala, John J. 1983. The origin of sound patterns in vocal tract constraints. In P. F. MacNeilage (ed.), *The production of speech*, 189–216. New York: Springer.

Ohala, John J. 1990. The phonetics and phonology of aspects of assimilation. In John Kingston & Mary Beckman (eds.), *Papers in laboratory phonology I: Between the grammar and physics of speech*, 258–275. Cambridge: Cambridge University Press.

Ohala, John J., Catherine P. Browman & Louis M. Goldstein. 1986. Towards an articulatory phonology. *Phonology* 3. 219–252. DOI:10.1017/S0952675700000658

Oudeyer, Pierre-Yves. 2006. *Self-organization in the evolution of speech*. Vol. 6. Oxford: OUP Oxford.

Peperkamp, Sharon, Rozenn Le Calvez, John-Pierre Nadal & Emmanuel Dupoux. 2006. The acquistion of allophonic rules: Statistical learning with linguistic constraints. *Cognition* 101. B31–B41. DOI:10.1016/j.cognition.2005.10.006

Peterson, Gordon E. & Ilse Lehiste. 1960. Duration of syllable nuclei in English. *The Journal of the Acoustical Society of America* 32(6). 693–703. DOI:10.1121/1.1908183

Phillips, Betty S. 1984. Word frequency and the actuation of sound change. *Language* 60(2). 320–342.

Pierrehumbert, Janet B. 2001. Exemplar dynamics: Word frequency, lenition and contrast. In Joan Bybee & Paul Hopper (eds.), *Frequency effects and the emergence of linguistic structure*, 137–158. Amsterdam: John Benjamins.

Pierrehumbert, Janet B. 2002. Word-specific phonetics. In Carlos Gussenhoven & Natasha Warner (eds.), *Laboratory phonology VII*, 101–139. Berlin: Mouton de Gruyter.

Pierrehumbert, Janet B., Forrest Stonedahl & Robert Daland. 2014. *A model of grassroots changes in linguistic systems*. https://arxiv.org/abs/1408.1985v1. arXiv preprint:1408.1985.

Prince, Alan & Paul Smolensky. 2004. *Optimality Theory: Constraint interaction in generative grammar*. Malden, MA: Blackwell Publishing.

Raphael, Lawrence J. 1972. Preceding vowel duration as a cue to the perception of the voicing characteristic of word-final consonants in American English. *The Journal of the Acoustical Society of America* 51(4B). 1296–1303.

Raymond, William D., Robin Dautricourt & Elizabeth Hume. 2006. Word-internal /t,d/ deletion in spontaneous speech: Modeling the effects of extra-linguistic, lexical, and phonological factors. *Language Variation and Change* 18(1). 55–97. DOI:10.1017/S0954394506060042

Repp, Bruno H., Alvin M. Liberman, Thomas Eccardt & David Pesetsky. 1978. Perceptual integration of acoustic cues for stop, fricative, and affricate manner. *Journal of Experimental Psychology: Human Perception and Performance* 4(4). 621–637.

Rosch, Eleanor. 1977. *Human categorization.* Vol. 1 (Studies in cross-cultural psychology). London: Academic Press.

Saltzman, Elliot L. & Kevin G. Munhall. 1989. A dynamical approach to gestural patterning in speech production. *Ecological Psychology* 1(4). 333–382. DOI:10.1207/s15326969eco0104_2

Scarborough, Rebecca A. 2004. *Coarticulation and the structure of the lexicon.* UCLA dissertation.

Schwartz, Geoffrey. 2010. Phonology in the speech signal-Unifying cue and prosodic licensing. *Poznań Studies in Contemporary Linguistics* 46(4). 499–518. DOI:doi.org/10.2478/v10010-010-0025-3

Solé, Maria-Josep. 1992. Phonetic and phonological processes: The case of nasalization. *Language and Speech* 35(1–2). 29–43. DOI:10.1177/002383099203500204

Sóskuthy, Márton. 2015. Understanding change through stability: A computational study of sound change actuation. *Lingua* 163. 40–60. DOI:10.1016/j.lingua.2015.05.010

Sóskuthy, Márton. 2013. *Phonetic biases and systemic effects in the actuation of sound change.* The University of Edinburgh dissertation.

Sóskuthy, Márton. 2014. *Explaining lexical frequency effects: A critique and an alternative account.* Paper presented at the 3rd Biennial Workshop on Sound Change: "Sound Change in Interacting Human Systems", May 28–31, at the University of California at Berkeley.

Stanford, James N. & Laurence A. Kenny. 2013. Revisiting transmission and diffusion: An agent-based model of vowel chain shifts across large communities. *Language Variation and Change* 25(2). 119–153. DOI:10.1017/S0954394513000069

Steels, Luc. 2005. The emergence and evolution of linguistic structure: From lexical to grammatical communication systems. *Connection Science* 17(3-4). 213–230. DOI:10.1080/09540090500269088

Steriade, Donca. 1995. Markedness and underspecification. In John A. Goldsmith (ed.), *The handbook of phonological theory*, 114–175. Cambridge, MA: Blackwell.

Stetson, Raymond H. 1928. *Motor phonetics: A study of speech movements in action.* Dordrecht: Springer. DOI:10.1007/978-94-015-3356-0

Surendran, Dinoj & Partha Niyogi. 2006. Quantifying the functional load of phonemic oppositions, distinctive features, and suprasegmentals. In Ole Nedergaard Thomsen (ed.), *Competing models of linguistics change: Evolution and beyond*, 43–58. Amsterdam: Benjamins.

Sweet, Henry. 1880. *A handbook of phonetics* (Clarendon Press Series). London: MacMillan & Co.

Tilsen, Sam. 2009. Subphonemic and cross-phonemic priming in vowel shadowing: Evidence for the involvement of exemplars in production. *Journal of Phonetics* 37(3). 276–296.

Tranel, Bernard. 1981. *Concreteness in generative phonology: Evidence from French.* Berkeley, CA: University of California Press.

Tupper, Paul F. 2014. Exemplar dynamics and sound merger in language. *SIAM Journal on Applied Mathematics* 75 (4). 1469–1492. DOI:10.1137/140998408

Turnbull, Rory. 2015. *Assessing the listener-oriented account of predictability-based phonetic reduction.* The Ohio State University dissertation.

Warren, Richard M. 1970. Perceptual restoration of missing speech sounds. *Science* 167(3917). 392–393. DOI:10.1126/science.167.3917.392

Wedel, Andrew. 2004. Category competition drives contrast maintenance within an exemplar-based production/perception loop. In John Goldsmith & Richard Wicentowski (eds.), *Proceedings of the seventh meeting of the ACL special interest group in computational phonology*, 1–10.

Wedel, Andrew. 2006. Exemplar models, evolution and language change. *The Linguistic Review* 23. 247–274. DOI:10.1515/TLR.2006.010

Wedel, Andrew. 2007. Feedback and regularity in the lexicon. *Phonology* 24. 147–185. DOI:10.1017/S0952675707001145

Wedel, Andrew. 2012. Lexical contrast maintenance and the organization of sublexical contrast systems. *Language and Cognition* 4 (4). 319–355. DOI:10.1515/langcog-2012-0018

Wedel, Andrew & Ibrahim Fatkullin. 2017. Category competition as a driver of category contrast. *Journal of Language Evolution* 2(1). 77–93. DOI:10.1093/jole/lzx009

Wedel, Andrew, Abby Kaplan & Scott Jackson. 2013. High functional load inhibits phonological contrast loss: A corpus study. *Cognition* 128(2). 179–186. DOI:10.1016/j.cognition.2013.03.002

Weinreich, Uriel, William Labov & Maivin Herzog. 1968. Empirical foundations for a theory of language change. In Winfred Lehmann & Yakov Malkiel (eds.), *Directions for historical linguistics*, 95–188. Austin, TX: University of Texas Press.

Wells, John C. 1982. *Accents of English*. Vol. 1. Cambridge: Cambridge University Press.

Yu, Alan C. L. 2013. Individual differences in socio-cognitive processing and the actuation of sound changes. In A. C. L. Yu (ed.), *Origins of sound change: Approaches to phonologization*, 201–227. Oxford: Oxford University Press.

Zsiga, Elizabeth C. 2000. Phonetic alignment constraints: Consonant overlap and palatalization in English and Russian. *Journal of Phonetics* 28 (1). 69–102. DOI:10.1006/jpho.2000.0109

Name index

Subject index